The Logic of Steel

To Hug, my enemy, for taking that neck cut on the forearm . . .

To Ted, my father, for finding him on the side of the road, and finding me a lawyer . . .

To Tony, my brother, for fronting me the money to cover the fine and the restitution.

Thanks, guys.

The Logic of Steel

A Fighter's View of Blade and Shank Encounters

James LaFond

Paladin Press
Boulder, Colorado

Also by James LaFond:

The Fighting Edge

The Logic of Steel: A Fighter's View of Blade and Shank Encounters
by James LaFond

Copyright © 2001 by James LaFond

ISBN 1-58160-130-1
Printed in the United States of America

Published by Paladin Press, a division of
Paladin Enterprises, Inc.
Gunbarrel Tech Center
7077 Winchester Circle
Boulder, Colorado 80301 USA
+1.303.443.7250

Direct inquiries and/or orders to the above address.

PALADIN, PALADIN PRESS, and the "horse head" design
are trademarks belonging to Paladin Enterprises and
registered in United States Patent and Trademark Office.

Visit our Web site at www.paladin-press.com

Contents

Acknowledgments

The book you are about to read was made possible by the cooperation of the following people: Banno, Rick Wayne, Iggy, Duncan, Raphael, Dan Funk, Link Sanchez, Laura, Tuck, Tattoo Rick, Ricky Mason, Haynes, Kenneth, Rich, Bryant, Suzy, Duke, Liz, Tony, Alain Burrese, Pepper, Rob, Faith, Brian, Spider, Sue, Mark Duszinski, Wally, Ted, Gary, Jason, Steve, Ben, Snookie, Boss John, Little Cindy, Brett, Ken, Roger, George, Dietz, Mike, Officer Lee, Robert, Joe Feely, Al the Pimp, Tom and Vicky, Ron Bone, Paul, Kirk, Dave the Cop, Dodge, Manny, Bernie, Puppet, Rob Mills, Crazy Steve Newman, Jahn, Ralph, Mouse, Jen, Mark, Ralph Dorien, Walt, Jimmy, Manny, Lester, Tommy, Judy, SmackDaddy Jay, Easy Al, Donald, Mac the Narc, Yebitz "the Ugly," Sandman, YoMan, MumbleJack, Bubba Crank, Carol, Quin, Herb, Satchel, Krazee Shank KillPower, Ray Shaw, Ted and Pat LaFond, Sheri, Spin, Roy, Abrim, Sleepy, Sifu Arturo Gabriel, and Chuck Goetz, my training partner. With special thanks to Steve Newman, for being a stand-up guy and coming through in a pinch.

I have incorporated the following published accounts into this study:

- Chris Pfouts' interviews of Pepsi, Steve Pendleton, Critter (my favorite), K.C., James Mahaffey, and Mike, as well as Chris' own encounter with the thumb-sucking knifer, all from his book *True Tales of American Violence*, also from Paladin Press.
- Thirty-two incidents reported in the pages of the *Baltimore Sun* or broadcast by WBAL Radio and WJZ Television.

The other 217 encounters are courtesy of the people named above and the author.

Genesis

Age 6:   Grandma gave me a Popsicle. After eating the treat, I took the stick outside and sharpened it on the sidewalk. I thought it was a fine blade. Grandma took it away.

Age 14:   Dad brought home a pair of 5 1/2-inch sheath knives for my brother and me. They came with leather-like sheaths that slid onto your belt, with plastic antler-style handles. My brother and I felt like full-grown men, until Mother took the knives away.

Age 16:   I found a steel fence post and took it, along with a sledge, hacksaw, and file, to a coal pile in the woods, where I forged a crude bastard sword. It was a powerful blade, slicing 16 inches of sheet metal with a single stroke. The police eventually took it away.

Age 24:   A biker gave me a 7 1/2-inch Othello lock blade. It was a fine blade. His old lady had insisted that he give it away.

Age 27:   A local dope dealer paid four junkies to shank me. They got the wrong guy. He fought them, took more cuts than Caesar, and walked away.

Age 32:   A punk tried to draw his blade on me. I trapped his hand at the hip and pressed three knuckles against his lips. The next day he gave me his butterfly knife as a peace offering, and I finally put the Othello away.

Age 36:   There is still nothing quite like a blade, fine or not. Since boyhood, blade fighting has seemed a haunting riddle. But today I sense a brutal logic as old as our kind.

He was grabbed . . . and then stabbed. The first stroke did not go deep. He seized the dagger as the others drew their blades, defending himself for a time, trying to avoid the desperate overhand strokes of his attackers. But it was no use. Twenty-three men—politicians or not—with steel in their hands and hate in their hearts would not be stopped with two naked hands. As he slowed and the blades began to dig deep, he went down. Mortally wounded, he drew his toga over his head. They would not see Gaius Julius Caesar take his last breath.

So ended the most powerful man of his time: a man who had risen farther above the masses than any taken down by the most personal means available to his enemies.

The small blade has been man's constant companion from the dawn of prehistory through the twilight of the twenty-first century. From the palmed flint blade of the mammoth hunter to the folding lock blade of the American deer hunter, the blade remains the most personal weapon in our now vast arsenal and continues to be widely used.

The premise of this book is simple: that man, the consummate tool-using predator, will use the blade practically and effectively, without training, and in a manner that will reflect his state of mind—or no mind. Only when he begins to philosophize outside the framework of the violent act will he adopt to frivolous conventions. Thus, the proper study of blade use begins with the study of violence and survival.

Stopping to Smell the Roses in the Garden of Hate

Bubbles grabbed his stomach and went down to his knees screaming, "You stabbed me!" and he was looking at his stomach. Oh, that was such a great day. I've never seen anything so hilarious.

—Link Sanchez

This book is part of a project dedicated to faithfully presenting the nature of personal violence: focusing on the immediate causes, actual physical dynamics, and ramifications of violent encounters. An important part of this presentation is a limited form of oral history that I call "action biography," which permits the reader to become acquainted with the attitudes, character, and perspective of those who participated in the true tales told in the following pages.

After reviewing this manuscript, I fear some readers may come away with the false impression that we live in the midst of a barely contained race war. Although much of the violence depicted is interracial, and many of the protagonists express racist views or use racial slurs in telling their tales, I have no evidence to suggest that racial mayhem is a dominant—or even significant—part of the American violence scene.

Most violence occurs between unarmed, untrained individuals of the same sex and race. However, extreme acts perpetrated by groups and armed aggressors are more likely than ordinary brawls to pit members of various races and ethnic groups against one another. When you fight with or against a blade or a group, you are, more often than not, leaving the world of brawling behind for the starker reality shared by the hunter and the hunted.

When Kenneth, one of my personal heroes, describes himself as having become "a pure nigger" during the course of a life-or-death fight, he is speaking symbolically, not literally. It might pain me to quote him, but he is making the strongest possible point. Like a woman using her manicured nails to imitate the bared claws of a cat as a way of expressing her jealousy of another woman, Kenneth is raising the dreaded image of the feared black man—as mythologized by the liberal press and caricatured in racist propaganda—to describe how far beyond the point of civility that particular event pushed him.

I feel there is a need to accurately quote a person using slang or profanity to describe violence. Substituting the classic N-word, with the common contemporary black term "nigga" would have de-emphasized the point Kenneth was trying to make.

Violence is something that needs to be seen in the raw to be understood. Any attempt to do so that falls short of being offensive to the current dominant world view will most certainly lack depth and authenticity. Leave it to the martial arts industry and the social-ist utopians to put a pretty face on an ugly subject.

You are about to explore the practical application of hatred var-ied enough to make you mad, make you laugh, and make you won-der why. It ain't pretty, but I hope you like it.

—James LaFond
March 2001

Prologue

*The knife came out and pop!
He held it right here [behind
the right hip], stepped forward, buried it, and yanked it
out. It was over, baby! They
booked, and so did we.*
—Link Sanchez

Banno is about 5 feet 8 inches, 190 pounds, and strong enough to lift an engine block out from under the hood of a 1972 Chevy Impala. And he is one of those guys with no sense of personal space. He's got bad breath and an in-your-face knack for crude conversation. When he talks to you his left arm is wrapped around the back of your neck and his right thumb is hooked in his front pants pocket—just inches forward of where the hilt of his well-oiled balisong protrudes from the rear pocket of his unbelted jeans, riding low on his plumber's hips.

At the time of the following incident Banno had been home from 'Nam for about 10 years. Since that time he had managed to screw up his life in ways that would keep a half-dozen social workers busy for another decade. He blamed his lot in life on the war. But from what I know of his life, participation in a doomed crusade against communism could only have been an improvement. If nothing else, it kept him out of prison.

A WALK ON THE
UNDERSIDE WITH BANNO

Incident #: 13-8
Time of occurrence: night
Duration: 8–10 seconds
Person relating story: first-person defender

It was a dark, damp night in "The District."
Banno had just emerged from the back room of a
bar after smoking more than his share of "some
good shit." He was stoned and hungry, with three
dollars left in his pocket. There was only one thing
to do: head down the street for the convenience store
in search of a bar of peanut-brittle candy. Banno
pulled on his windbreaker and headed outside.

The bar entrance was at the base of a narrow
stairwell. Since Banno liked to appear careless (but
was actually paranoid), he carelessly shut the door
behind him before checking the stairs. He found
himself face-to-face with a tall black man (and,
based on his appearance and mannerisms, quite
obviously a heroin addict) wearing a trench coat.
The black man flipped a switchblade out to his right
and held his left hand out to the side in a "give me"
gesture, and demanded, "Give me yo money."

Banno wasn't about to lose his last three bucks
to some junkie—not when he had the munchies!
Banno said, "OK," as he reached for his rear right
pants pocket (where many male robbery victims
keep their wallets but where Banno kept his Filipino
blade). When he got his palm on the balisong,
Banno said to the would-be thief, "That's the stu-
pidest thing you ever did."

This macho statement appeared to stun the
addict—his mouth fell open, his eyes bulged, and
his left hand stopped motioning for cash—as Banno

deployed the blade in a brief whirl behind his hip and plunged it into the taller man's left breast. According to Banno, "The dumb bastard just stood there and stared at me—so I stuck 'um again."

Each time that Banno struck (with a pronated saber grip), he buried the 5-inch blade up to the hilt. After the second stab, Banno noticed that the light-gray trench coat was growing darker around the chest. "After the second one the trench coat got dark, and it spread like this [spreads fingers of right hand over left chest]."

When the would-be robber continued to stand and stare in apparent shock, Banno stabbed him a third time. "What else am I supposed to do? I was taught to finish strong.

"At this point he started to weave. So I stepped to the side [right] and let 'um fall."

As the black man fell face-first off the bottom stair into the base of the stairwell, Banno walked up the stairs—pocketing his blade on the way—and headed down the street at a walk.

"I was real hungry—feelin' pretty good. Was late gettin' home."

Banno stopped at the convenience store, got his candy, and then headed home, where he "played with the kids."

Banno doesn't watch the news or read the paper, and he never went back to that bar again. Not only did he not know whether the man in the stairwell had died, he didn't care. He was incredulous when I remarked that I would have read the police blotter at the first opportunity to determine if I was in any danger. He calmly replied, "But I wasn't worried about him. He was no longer a danger."

Based on the location and penetration of the wounds, and the fact that the streets in that part of town are notoriously lacking in Good Samaritans, I classified this episode as an armed aggressor fatality—an exceedingly rare outcome.

Banno never killed again, as far as I know, but he also never learned how to stay out of trouble and ended up doing time for various unrelated crimes.

Banno may be a crude, uncivilized dude, but it could be argued that he did civilization a favor when he plugged that dope fiend. Unfortunately, the person getting stabbed in such a manner is more often an innocent victim than a thieving degenerate. Worst of all, the "civilized modern society" that Banno unwittingly did a small part to protect is steadily eroding the individual's right to self-defense. The most glaring example is the constant liberal assault on the Second Amendment.

However, the antigun movement in the United States is only the most recent manifestation of modern man's misunderstanding of personal violence. Since the latter half of the 19th century, the man who wields a knife in defense has been as much a pariah as the felon who misuses a firearm.

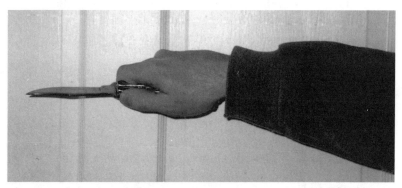

Banno's preferred fighting grip: a pronated (turned horizontal) saber grip (thumb used to guide rather than grasp), which deploys the shoulder muscle—much like a boxer's cross—and permits the blade to slip between the enemy's ribs. The knife in this photo is a cheap version of Banno's beloved weapon—the Filipino balisong knife—and was given to the author as a peace offering by a young man who had attempted to draw on him the day before.

There is nothing more terrifying to the soft body and weak mind of the modern gender-neutral person than the thought of butchering—or being butchered by—a face-to-face antagonist. This is a fear as old as man, rooted in the terror of the leopard's claw and the hyena's jaw, and reflected quite adequately in modern horror films. The blade, too, is as old as man—an imitation of the predator's claw or fang—and consequently (as well as mechanically) offers the most personal form of protection and violation in the modern arsenal.

When used effectively, the knife is even more personal than the fist. Regrettably, even the most basic facets of attack and defense regarding stabbing and cutting weapons are entirely missed by the vast majority of modern self-defense practitioners—a deficiency this book seeks to redress.

CHAPTER 1

The Real Raw Deal

Understanding Blade and Shank Use

*I tell you what. I scared to
death of a knife. I ratha have a
muthafuca shoot me.*

—Duke

STEEL SIDE SHANK

Incident #42-2
Time of occurrence: day
Duration: 10–15 seconds
Perspective: eyewitness

Charles was arguing with an inmate from another cell block when the other inmate put his right hand beneath his coveralls and drew a shank (a 6-inch length of sharpened sheet-metal cuttings bound with duct tape) close to his body, cocked it next to his ribs, and lunged for Charles' belly. Charles threw his hips back and his arms high to the sides as he hopped back to avoid the stab. He recovered in time to push the knifer back by his shoulders. As he pushed off, Charles turned to run. He should have looked back before running to the stairs.

The knifer flipped his shank over to the "ice-

pick" grip and pursued at full speed, as the other
inmates gave way. As Charles hit the top step and
began his descent, the knifer plunged the shank into
his upper back. He did this three times before
Charles hit the second step. The two continued
down the stairs—ever slower. On the second and
third step Charles took between five and seven additional stabs to his shoulders. On the fourth step
Charles sustained three to five additional stabs as
his legs began to buckle. When they hit the landing,
Charles collapsed and was stabbed about five more
times. At this point, the knifer looked the eyewitness
(who was standing on the landing) "square in the
eye" and calmly slid his shank beneath his coveralls
and walked off. Within seconds all the inmates in
the cell block—except for Charles and his
assailant—were detained and searched by guards.

The above encounter was related to me by Raphael, a martial
artist who has survived gang fights, bar brawls, street fights, prize
fights, and knife fights. He has worked as a doorman, an enforcer,
and a corner man. Of the dozens of tough, experienced street fighters I have interviewed, he is among the most experienced (he does-
n't know how many fights he's been in, but some day—when I'm
done picking his brain—I'll let him know) and is certainly the most
versatile, holding advanced ranks in six fighting arts. I've trained
with him, drunk with him, broken bread with him, and once kept him
from stomping a teenaged "wannabe G" into the asphalt.

Now, why have I devoted an entire paragraph to describing the
toughness and experience of this eyewitness? Because he was scared
breathless and wilted under the glare of the prison knifer. Raphael
will fight anybody, for almost any reason, but he's not stupid. He
was looking into the eyes of a heartless predator and didn't waste a
moment dreaming up a martial arts fantasy defense.

That's a lesson I won't forget. Raphael has gone empty-handed
against a knifer, and he knew not to go there with *this* guy. To be able
to avoid, or possibly fight, such people we must first know how they

operate and how to spot them. The knifer should be out of prison by now, and I could run into him—or someone like him—on the bus tonight. If so, I won't even have to look to know he's there. When the junior gangstas in the back of the bus stop chattering like so many birds in the jungle, I'll know the predator is there: sitting in the left corner of the back bench seat. When he slinks out the back door, their adolescent threats will start filling the bus again. . . .

Did Charles Have a Chance?

Raphael and I determined the timeframe and approximate number of stabs based on our reenacting the encounter in his living room. Time perception is one of the first things to go when you are that close to serious violence. Since Charles didn't die and there was no legal action, the number of wounds was not made known.

The stabbing of Charles actually represents two distinct attempts at weapon use. The knifer initially used his weapon from a *ready posture*, with the knife retracted in the rear hand, as do most knifers. Had he cornered Charles, he would certainly have persisted with this tactic. Charles' flight triggered a more predatory action, in the form of the running back stab, a crude but effective tactic.

The oddest thing about this incident was that both parties were the same size. Usually the man with the weapon is smaller or at least shorter. Charles (like the knifer) was large and athletic and initially did well once the knife had been drawn. However, he knew he would be cut and decided to buy his 30 seconds (until the guards showed) by running. This was really a good choice. He only made two mistakes:

1. A shanker is more likely to give chase than is a typical knifer. Since the best way to stab on the run is with an overhand grip, a shanker who adopts this grip is clearly indicating that he will give chase. Charles should have looked back and either fought (he had done all right when the knifer was using a more practical grip) or altered his course.
2. When fleeing from an aggressor who appears to have approximately your level of athletic ability (Charles and the knifer were described as identical in build), *never* descend a flight of stairs.

Climb the stairs or run in circles if need be, but never give your pursuer the option of diving on your back or dragging you down by the shoulders.

Having made these two points, we—as self-defense students and teachers—must refrain from criticizing a defender such as Charles who chooses a reasonable course of action but fails to make two small calculations while under the kind of pressure most of us have never faced. Did you know about the significance of the overhand knife posture in the context of a chase? Did you know that running *down* the stairs was a trap?

Consider Charles' struggle—in the context he was forced to live it—to learn from his misfortune. Don't assume that some knife-sparring experience, or the use of a specialized fighting stance on your part, would put an attacker of the type that Charles faced at a crucial disadvantage.

• • •

Approximately one of every ten violent acts involves the use of a cutting or stabbing weapon. Although such weapons are among the most deadly and are the preferred tool of the lone male felon, in their practical application they are the least understood of all weapons.

To comprehend the use of edged weapons we must grasp their mechanics and potential. What are the options available to the blade or shank user? What are his limitations?

Numero uno is the fact that a person in possession of an *unde-ployed* weapon is *not* armed. When I interview a man who engaged in a fistfight but did not draw his folder, I classify him as unarmed. Knives don't cut people. *People* use knives to cut people. An object does not become a weapon until it is deployed.

I have analyzed the edged-weapon encounters I have experienced, witnessed, and collected by the following categories:

- Weapon
- Use
- Posture

WEAPON

The first way I decided to slice this grisly pie was to break down the action according to weapon type. This permitted me to relate the uses, use postures, injury patterns, and legal risks associated with the deployment of various tools. When it comes to the study of real blade fighting, "tool" is the appropriate term for almost all weapons used in combat. Virtually all edged weapons are misused household or workplace tools, *not* deliberately crafted weapons.

This remains true even when one considers the major knife category. Just about every piece of steel that is used in the commission of a violent crime, or is grabbed to turn the tide of a brawl, would be classified as worthless junk by any self-respecting knife enthusiast, dealer, or schooled knife fighter. I have grouped edged weapons into four broad categories (in part so I can stop using the term *edged weapon*).

Edged-Weapon Types

1. Razors—straight razors, box cutters, utility knives, and loose razor blades
2. Shanks—any improvised stabbing implement, including pens, corkscrews, ice picks, and object used to pry open paint cans or shellfish.
3. Knives—all folding knives and daggers, kitchen cutlery, and sheath knives smaller than a Bowie
4. Swords—antiques, replicas, Bowies, machetes, sickles

Top-quality weapons are rarely used in real fights. Even such marginal quality weapons as my 20-year-old Bowie—which I use to cut down trees and butcher hams—account for less than 4 percent of the weapons identified in this study. The incidence of high-quality blade use is statistically zero!

Now, let's put a price tag on the most common weapons in the knifer's arsenal: box cutter, $1.25; utility knife, $1.99; pencil, 15 cents; 3 1/2- to 4-inch folding lock blade, $5.00.

Perhaps the only redeeming quality demonstrated by your neighborhood knifer is that he is a conservative investor.

The straight razor is the weapon most likely to be used to inflict a pressure cut (slice). It is the blade preferred by black women. Cost: approximately $3.00.

The aptly named screwdriver, the Darth Vader of shanks, is the preferred weapon of the impoverished male sociopath. Cost: approximately $1.99.

The butcher knife is the weapon of choice of the white working-class woman. Cost: approximately $4.39.

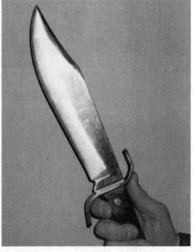

A classic Bowie knife is classified for this study as a sword. The use of a Bowie has not been documented. Swords and sword-like knives are used almost exclusively by white males at or near their home or vehicle. Cost: approximately $40.00.

Edged-Weapon Trends

My study of violence in general, and of armed encounters of all kinds, has led to the identification of three trends that are present with the use of all weapons, but are most pronounced in regards to cutting and stabbing weapons.

1. Material—people are being butchered with junk.
2. Menace—the more menacing a weapon appears, the more likely it will be used to threaten instead of injure and the more likely the brandishing or use will bring legal penalties.
3. Fear of failure—a weapon user who fears that his tool will not menace effectively or that it will fail him in combat is more likely to act with extreme ruthlessness and less likely to pay a legal penalty for his crime . . . so long as the act does not produce a body.

The following table demonstrates my methodology and seeks to answer an age-old question. You be the judge.

IS THE PEN(CIL) MIGHTIER THAN THE SWORD?

| Weapon | Times Deployed | Injury Attempts | ARMED PARTY | | ANTAGONIST | | |
			Wound	Legal	Armed	Wound	Death
Pencil	7	100%	none	14%	none	100%	14%
Sword	11	55%	9%	64%	27%	27%	9%

This comparison asks as many questions as it answers.

- The situations?
  –One hundred percent of the pencilers were acting as the aggressor.
  –Forty-five percent of the swordsmen were acting as the aggressor.
  –(Aggression is the second most important advantage in any violent altercation, experience being the most important.)

- State-of-mind?
  –Fifty-five percent of the swordsmen were drunk. (Look at the injury attempts.)
  –None of the pencilers were drunk.

- The deaths?
  –Through the left eye with a full-length sharpened #2 pencil.
  –Decapitation with a katana (samurai sword).

- The perpetrators?
  –The swordsmen were all adult males.
  –The pencilers were primarily adolescent males.

(If I accomplish nothing else in the pursuit of this knife study, I should at least manage to elevate the status of the lowly "twerp"—that half-pint wannabe with his hand in his pocket and his nose out of joint—as an armed antagonist.)

- Setting?
  –Sixty-four percent of the swordsmen were in their home or on their porch.
  –Eighty-six percent of the pencilers were in high school or behind bars.
  –The sword is used primarily as a home-defense weapon and as an ego booster by eccentric drunken men. By contrast, the pencil is a device employed by a stealthy or opportunistic aggressor within a restricted setting. Confrontation versus predation.

USE

Holding

Holding a weapon during an altercation, without showing it or bringing it into play, is a rare—but viable—option. I was once attacked by a large drunk who began shoving me around. When I got my feet planted, I decided to fight but didn't want to make it a knife fight. I drew my utility knife below his line of sight and began to throw it across the floor so that neither one of us would be tempted to use it. (I had been working with it, and it was sticking out of my belt where either one of us could get to it if we went to the floor.)

As I was beginning to toss the blade, my attacker started to bear down on me with a clenched fist, and I automatically flipped the blade over to the reverse grip and held it under his beer gut. I knew

I would cut him despite my desire not to. We stood eye-to-eye as he growled obscenities and cocked his right hand for a cross. I simply met his stare until he lost his nerve. He didn't even know I had the blade ready until a bystander mentioned it afterward.

I believe I won that stare-down because my eyes reflected the confidence I felt based on his impending surgery, which would have begun when I ducked his big right hand. He was shaken by the eye contact and soon apologized and withdrew the fight challenge he had issued earlier.

There is also a lesson to be learned from the drunk's failure to realize that a blade was inches from his intestines. This is an obvious case of stress-induced tunnel vision. Be careful about harnessing your hatred within reach of an unseen hand.

Showing

Showing, or brandishing, is a common use of the blade. Showing works better when an effective looking weapon is employed. This is a risky visual threat that reflects fear and desperation and is generally the knifer's most defensive act short of running. However, this is not always the case.

Showing a blade may be the prelude to an attack, an attempt to demoralize you and soften you up for the kill. This is most often the case when the blade is shown to you when you are cornered or is shown by a member of a group.

I was once working with a real pack of degenerates on the night crew of a brand-new mega-supermarket. We were aptly nicknamed "The Dirty Dozen" by our dapper absentee taskmaster. At the time I was taking three buses through the city, was experiencing back problems, and had not yet learned the local dialects and body language. So I was packing my Othello in my back pocket concealed by a draped bandanna or a flannel shirt wrapped around the waist. This was obviously not an effective concealment method, because at least one of my co-workers knew I was armed.

We were in the lunchroom with two deli girls when Jet, the 300-pound porter, walked through to the bathroom, where it was his habit to perch, grunt, and cheer himself on as he hollered for Mole, an 80-pound midget, to come and assist him.

Mole normally took this kind of abuse in stride, but he was in love with the hotdog girl. In an attempt to impress her, Mole grabbed his trusty case cutter, kicked open the men's room door, kicked open the stall door, and said, "Shut up."

This was followed by the sound of his case cutter clattering across the floor, and Jet's voice booming with laughter. Mole marched out of the men's room in a rage, walked up to where I was seated next to his beloved, looked me square in the eye, held out his hand, and demanded, "Give me your knife."

I drew the utility knife and held it out. He shook his head, pointed to my right hip, and said, "No, the big one."

I looked at my partner, Nate, who knew these guys well, and he gave me the go-ahead. When I pulled the Othello from its sheath, one of the guys said, "That's illegal." Mole (who bathed infrequently) licked his crusty lips and worked his fingers expectantly.

When I fully deployed the blade, the hotdog girl screamed and jumped off her seat. The room went silent as Nate corrected the earlier commentator by remarking, "No, that's ridiculous!" As I flipped the blade around to hand it over hilt first, Mole stood before me like a prince ready to receive the royal scepter of power: right hand extended, eyes wide and bulging, body perched tensely on the tips of his little toes.

When Mole grasped the hilt he was transformed to such a degree that I was already preparing my defense for the accessory-to-murder charge. He marched like a maniac, knife in hand (it truly looked like a sword in his hand) toward the men's room door—from where Jet could still be heard yelling for his pink Cottonelle. As the crew shrank back uneasily. Mole looked like a killer, transformed by his first taste of power after 40 lonely years as the butt of countless jokes. He kicked the door with such authority that he had to parry it with the blade as it bounced back at him.

Jet grew silent as the sound of the heavy door slamming echoed through the store. We all listened tensely for Mole's epiphany—his defining moment as an ascendant human being. He kicked open the stall door and yelled, "Now, fat boy!"

Jet, obviously still perched on the throne of his putrid little kingdom, began to cry barely audible apologies, as Mole coached him, "Yeah, there we go, that's more like it, right on, fat boy."

As the lunchroom roared with laughter Mole marched up to me,

The author's Othello lock blade, partially deployed. It is held "edge out" in the manner promoted by Filipino and eclectic knife fighting styles. This is the manner in which the author prefers to grip a blade in the overhand because it permits a powerful—though limited-arc—slash. However, there is no record of a blade's being used to slash in this fashion.

The author's Othello lock blade fully deployed and held in the saber grip— with the thumb acting as a guide rather than a stabilizer. Although the author prefers a natural, fully grasped "hatchet" or "hammer" grip, this particular blade feels best when held like a thrusting sword.

saluted—his heels smacking smartly together—returned the weapon, puffed out his chest, and said, "Thank you, Mr. Rambo." Nate and I were so impressed with his valor that we got him drunk and arranged for him to be assaulted by a stripper at a local club.

WARNING constitutes touching the antagonist or victim with the weapon, without the intent or effect of injuring. The most common use of this tactic is a strong-arm robber's holding a knife to the victim's throat while demanding cash. A less common method can best be illustrated by an encounter that happened within a month of the Mole saga.

Nate didn't really like me, but he liked drinking with me. He was large and sociable, with a reputation for winning fights. That made him a magnet for tough guys who wanted to brag about losing to him—and maybe to sue him to boot. I was small and antisocial, with a reputation for not winning, not quitting, and using a blade to avoid losing. I was tough-guy repellent. Bragging about pounding some bone-rack into the ground is not worth getting shanked over.

My lack of social status also made me a good diplomat. I had rrecently saved Nate from Russel, a menacing career felon who insisted on fighting over the bar tab. My offer to stand in for Nate or pay the tab threw Russel into crisis mode, as he considered how oafish he would look chasing me around the pool table. He had built his reputation—and self-image—on ripping apart other heavy-weights, not stomping "shorties."

So when a tough guy started picking a fight with Nate, the day after he got out of jail for hospitalizing three punks, he looked to me hopefully.

I was 3 feet behind Mr. Tough Guy when Nate gave me that "I don't want to get locked up tonight" look.

I was down on my left knee, tying my shoe when I decided to act. As I stood, I drew the blade low and locked it out below my right knee. The click of the blade lock froze Mr. Tough Guy. He was squared off, facing Nate with his feet slightly more than shoulder-width apart.

The moment he froze I slashed up between his legs, hitting him in the testicles with the *back* of the blade. He lunged for his family jewels with both hands, pivoted right 180 degrees, and stared at me in bug-eyed horror, as I slid the blade behind my belt buckle. He then hobbled at full speed—with both hands

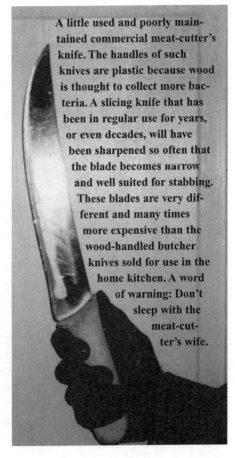

A little used and poorly maintained commercial meat-cutter's knife. The handles of such knives are plastic because wood is thought to collect more bacteria. A slicing knife that has been in regular use for years, or even decades, will have been sharpened so often that the blade becomes narrow and well suited for stabbing. These blades are very different and many times more expensive than the wood-handled butcher knives sold for use in the home kitchen. A word of warning: Don't sleep with the meat-cutter's wife.

cupping his testicles—for a block, until he ducked around the corner, presumably to make a gender check.

Nate looked at me in amazement and asked, You didn't?"

I drew the blade and "cut" across my left wrist with the back of the blade. He almost broke a rib laughing.

Parrying

Parrying with the balde is theoretically possible, but the only example I can cite is Mole's defending against the men's room door in 1993. However, there have been effective parries (blocks) against the blade with improvised weapons. The small size of the most modern blades makes it more practical to strike the opponent's blade hand than to touch his blade with yours. In any case, parrying is most properly discussed in the context of blade-to-blade or blade-to-blunt weapon situations, both of which are extremely rare. One-sided armed encounters are the rule, not the exception.

This piece of junk is a $7 machete, which can only be used effectively to slash and hack. This is a very common civilian weapon in the Caribbean or in any area with sugar cane plantations. It is good for showing because its sword-like appearance has a demoralizing effect. As a weapon it is most often used to disable, not kill. Its mechanics are identical to those of the stick.

Pummeling

Pummeling is another sword tactic that is possible with a knife, but it has not been documented in my violence survey. The backhand strike with the base of your weapon's handle (the pommel) certainly sounds like a good idea, and works in training when in close contact, but I have no knowledge of this tactic's actually being used.

Slicing

Slicing, or pressure cutting, is a rare method of lacerating people, most common with razors since they are not reliable impact weapons. This is the method used by meat cutters, who carry their own razor-sharp blades back and forth to work because they don't like novices messing with their tools. I once read a *Reader's Digest* story about a butcher who was mauled by a bear but managed to kill it with a handheld arrow. He credited his knowledge of animal anatomy gained in the meat room with saving his life. Again, he used pressure-cutting tactics.

Although the antique bayonet and sharpened screwdriver are the most effective stabbing implements, the most common effective stabbing weapon is the folding lock blade that has a thumbing point, which permits a secure saber grip (a grip used by unschooled knifers who don't know what it's called) and prevents the hand from slipping onto the blade on impact.

Slashing

Slashing, or impact cutting, is one of the three most common uses of the blade (the other two being showing and stabbing). Asian swords and sword-type weapons (e.g., machetes, sickles, Bowies, kukris) are primarily—if not exclusively—designed for slashing or hacking.

Stabbing

Stabbing, or thrusting, is the most lethal method of blade use and is the only viable way to use a shank. With the exception of the utility knife, no razor is even marginally suited for stabbing.

Defining Weapons from the User's Perspectives

I know I cut you, but you stuck me! When you hear about people getting killed, you don't hear about them dying from getting cut; you hear about them dying from getting stabbed!

—Chuck Goetz,
on knife sparring

When the definition of your subject matter virtually defies description, it's a safe bet that the actual study is going to be somewhat less difficult. (Yeah, that's what I said, *less difficult.*) I had such a hard time defining what an edged weapon was that, by the time I got around to studying its use, I had already sorted out most of the loose ends.

The problem with defining edged-weapon use is that the definition becomes so broad. You can cut somebody with just about anything, whether it's edged or not. An octagonal nunchaku will cut, and so will a shovel or a ceramic beer mug. This definition for an edged weapon is used by Steve Tarani, the senior edged-weapon instructor for Gunsite Training Center in Arizona: "Any object that is capable of cutting, puncturing, or tearing flesh."

This is a classic forensic definition of a weapon. The problem with such weapon definitions—related to their actual use—is that they reflect the perspective of the victim and those who have to clean up and explain the resulting mess. This brings us full circle to the narrow defender-as-main-actor perspective that seems to dominate the whole field of self-defense. How can the rational mind be obsessed constantly with the role of the defender when one is studying aggression?!

Sorry, folks, but when it comes to aggression the aggressor takes center stage. In light of this reality, I define a weapon based on the following two factors:

1. The weapon's primary capacity—firearm, edged, blunt (a shovel is more blunt than edged)
2. The user's practical and emotional relationship to the weapon

For example, though a knife has a blunt-force capacity if one strikes with the butt, butting is not the commonly recognized means by which one injures or kills with a knife. Likewise, the man who uses a knife in a fight is not pinning his hopes on pummeling his way to victory. And, if he is a seafood clerk, he already has an ingrained practical relationship to his knife, which revolves around slicing.

This line of thought led me to exclude axes and hatchets from this study, primarily because I define tools that are not knife-like or do not have a primary cutting function as tools. Most weapons that fall into the tool category are blunt metallic objects that have corners and thus the capacity to cut. I could have categorized the few hatchets in the survey with the swords since their method of use is similar. But the guy who picks up a hatchet is hoping to break and crush his opponent's bones, not sever or skewer him. As John F. Gilbey so aptly put it, "After all, to a man whose only tool is a hammer, everything tends to look like a nail."

This began as a book on knives and knife-like weapons, and I aim to keep it that way. The edge—and the ability to cut and stab, as well as the menace associated with the brandishing of something that is universally recognized as a cutting or thrusting weapon—is the primary consideration.

The secondary consideration is that the weapon is used like a knife. The knife is central. It is the original edged weapon, which inspired the sword, the razor, and the use of shanks. Every punk stabbing away with a pencil wishes he had a knife in his hand.

I have classified bottles as "common items" because the everyday relationship with such innocuous items sharply defines their use. But I have documented three cases in which a bottle was intentionally altered and used to cut, stab, or warn. I have included those bottles in this study as shanks or razors since they were redesigned (however hastily) and used as such. Normally the bottle is taken as is and used like a rock.

What the goon wants to do to you with his weapon is, oh, so important. Consider the assault rifle, our most extreme form of personal protection or (in the wrong hands) violation. It can be used as a blunt weapon or, if fixed with a bayonet, an edged weapon. If three guys broke into your ranch and you used your M14 to blast one, gore another, and cave in the skull of the third, we're talking about three very different types of weapon use.

POSTURE

When studying weapon use, the first consideration is the weapon, the second technique, and the third tactics. The primary indicator of likely tactics is the user's posture. Posture is the relationship the knifer forms with his weapon in the presence of an antagonist. It is his framework for action. The three aspects of the knifer's posture are these:

*   Grip
*   Orientation (which includes stance)
*   Action

Both traditional and eclectic artists tend to consider knife use from a similar reference point: the knifer's stance. However, a knifer's attack is usually facilitated by using a casual approach posture—not by taking a stance and challenging his victim. The knifer most often approaches at a walk with the right hand held close to the right hip.

My initial research into knife use led me to believe that the manner in which the knifer gripped his weapon and oriented himself in relation to an antagonist was a reliable indicator of his impending action or inaction.

The Overhand Posture

When I interview an aggressor, defender, or eyewitness to a blade altercation, my first question is how the weapon was gripped. If the interview is in person, I hand over my pen and ask for a demonstration. In most cases, unarmed or third parties do not pick up on such subtleties as thumb placement. However, everyone remembers a good Norman Bates imitation. So the first step of the process is determining if the knifer used an overhand grip, otherwise known as the reverse, false, or ice-pick grip.

Gripping a blade or shank in this manner so dictates the knifer's options that grip becomes the only consideration. The orientation of knifers using this grip is so dynamic and varied—and the incidence of such use so rare—that I go right to the action. I have documented four methods by which real knifers strike from the overhand posture. These are *not* the two methods depicted in self-defense magazines.

Fantasy Stroke 1

With the exception of one woman attempting to jump-stab a prone man, I have not documented a single case of a blade or shank's being used with a single full-commitment overhand down stroke, as depicted in virtually all traditional blade defense demonstrations.

Fantasy Stroke 2

I have not documented a single case of a blade's being used to slash in an inward "ripping" motion in the manner promoted by eclectic and Filipino martial artists.

The overhand posture is used exclusively against unarmed individuals in spontaneous situations. It is never a full-commitment stroke from the shoulder, but rather a short, chopping stroke from the elbow. It represents the rarest, most predatory, and most effective use of the blade, although its effectiveness has more to do with "situations" than "technique."

Downward Stroke

Also called the woodpecker, the downward stroke is the only stroke that has been used effectively on a fleeing target. However, it is not known to be lethal in such cases, since most such blows fall on the shoulder blades of larger individuals. This is the most common use of knives and shanks held in the overhand grip. This stroke is employed primarily as a series of multiple pursuit blows or stabs to the back and secondarily as a stab by a mounted defender.

Outward Stroke

The outward, or backhand, stroke is the second most deadly stroke and is only used by an intense aggressor. The only three one-stroke kills with a blade or shank known to the author were with this stroke. This is a lateral outward hammerfist executed while rising from a seated position or stepping obliquely toward the target, stabbing the face or chest.

Inward Stroke

The inward stroke, also known as the "baby Bates" or "kidney spike," is primarily a defensive close-quarter stabbing method aimed at the neck and kidneys. The more inward (as opposed to downward) the blow, the better the penetration. The only known offensive application of this grip was delivered below the ribs from behind with an upward twist.

Leading with the Knife

Once I have determined that the weapon was employed in some variation of the natural grip, my second question is, "Was the blade held *between* the knifer and the other party?" This is easy to determine unless the knifer was surrounded.

So what does this posture indicate? Just about everyone gets this wrong, even though it is the most easily explained posture. As with any act of armed aggression, there is a practical and or emotional explanation for the aggressor's action. Unfortunately, the study of blade use fosters many false assumptions.

Deadly Misconceptions

Few martial arts teachers have been involved in real altercations that involved a blade or shank. Nevertheless, they are often compelled to prepare their students to deal with such a situation. There are three basic foundations for teaching defenses against edge weapons:

1. Traditional artists base their defenses on a belief in the effectiveness of their fighting style. The underpinning concept is that the knifer is an inferior being who will be moving in slow motion relative to the lightning-fast techniques of the martial artist, permitting almost any antiblade defense to work. I'm thankful that this attitude is being eroded—a good thing since most of the resulting defenses are suicidal. However, misconceptions based on blind faith in martial artistry persist.

2. The eclectic approach is based largely on the influence of the Filipino blade and stick arts among American martial artists. Although these arts are priceless in that they debunk the traditional myths and arm the student with the basis for an effective defense through an acquaintance with the mechanics of the blade, they too foster misconceptions.

3. The military approach reflects pure ruthless practicality, revolving around the offensive use of a weapon designed for combat. This mind-set fosters two misconceptions: the principal one being that those who do not use the most effective methods will be ineffective in combat, followed by the one that says knife fights are fought with combat knives.

Each of the above blade-fighting foundations fosters a deadly myth, each corresponding to its preceding misconcption, regarding the lead posture:

Myth 1:   The traditional assumption is that this stance pre-
          cedes a full commitment lunge (the straw foes
          faced by the martial arts master must be depicted
          as incompetent)—an armor-piercing tactic that is
          centuries out of date.

Myth 2:   The eclectic assumption, born of sparring experi-
          ence, is that this is a fast boxing-type stance that
          is the basis for a low-commitment slashing
          attack. This reflects the mind-set of the duelist,
          who has developed great respect for the knife as
          a weapon. This assumption only holds true in
          limited circumstances. If the knifer has you cor-
          nered, is part of a group, or has a razor, you may
          expect such tactics.

Myth 3:   Modern military-style combat knife aficionados
          shrug off such knife deployments as laughable.
          However, the *lead* proved to be effective for
          defensive purposes in more than a dozen real
          altercations.

A knifer who places his weapon between himself and his antagonist is most likely engaged in simple brandishing. The more deadly the knife appears to be, the more likely this is an invitation to leave. The smaller the blade and the more crowded the circumstances, the more likely this will be a low-commitment slashing attack. Shanks are never used in this manner. Leading with the knife is the knifer's most defensive act—short of running.

The Ready Posture

Any knife deployment in which the knife is not gripped *overhand* and is not held in the *lead* is regarded as a *ready* posture. Eliminating the *overhand* and the *lead* results in a broad category of knife use that features concealment, protection, and retraction of the knife hand. A knife held to the side is regarded as held in the ready. With the exception of swords held in the *ready*, this posture indicates a desire not to show the blade, minimizing risks and maximizing results.

Integrated Tactics

Virtually all blade and shank altercations are one-dimensional: with an armed party using a single posture and technique against an unarmed party. Charles' jailhouse ordeal related at the beginning of this chapter was a rare exception. It's usually one way, all the way. Let's look at a very different incidence of integrated blade use.

BRO'S BLADE

Incident #39-19
Time of occurrence: day
Duration: 8-10 seconds
Perspective: first-person defender

At age 11, Raphael was playing baseball at a park in Chicago when a long-time rival, a large Polish kid named Allen, threatened him with a bat. (On a previous occasion Allen had stoned Raphael from a distance. They also had fought on a staircase at school, and Allen would eventually snipe at Raphael with a bow and arrow.)

Raphael drew his older brother's 5-inch switchblade from his rear right pants pocket and held it in the lead. He was confident but not confident enough to attack, and ended up circling as Allen proceeded to stalk him.

The leading draw was a defensive response, not indicating a desire to enter. As Raphael gained confidence he squared off (in the ready), bringing his ball glove up as a shield (he hadn't taken it off), and delivered his most sinister line, "I'm gonna cutch-you up, whiteboy." With that, bystanders began to encourage Raphael, and Allen backed off.

STATISTICAL BREAKDOWN
OF BLADE AND SHANK USES

In the above incident Raphael showed his weapon from two postures. The lead draw held Allen at bay, and going to the ready caused him to back down. The jailhouse knifer who did Charles stabbed with his shank from two different postures: unsuccessfully from the ready and successfully from the overhand.

Four men stabbing one man from the ready equals one act of violence, two parties, and four examples of weapon use. If each knifer dips his blade into the defender and he dies, then we have four lethal uses of the blade. If only one knifer is arrested or charged (very likely), then we only have one example of legalities associated with blade use.

BREAKDOWN OF 275 USES OF KNIFE BY WEAPON AND POSTURE (PERCENTAGES)

Weapon	Use	Injury Attempt	USER		ANTAGONIST		
			Legal	Medical	Armed	Medical	Death
Razor	15	68	33	3	10	55	3
Shank	11	93	40	10	7	83	27
Knife	70	67	30	10	20	60	15
Sword	4	50	67	8	25	42	8

Posture	Use	Injury Attempt	USER		ANTAGONIST		
			Legal	Medical	Armed	Medical	Death
Overhand	14	85	40	5	13	80	30
Lead	31	5%	26	6	31	35	1
Ready	55	78	33	11	11	71	17

CHAPTER 2

The Ignorant, the Arrogant, and the Unkind

Comprehending Violence and Armed Encounters

I twisted the knife until I heard his heart-strings sing.

—James Bowie

WE TAKE IT ALL

Incident #50-05
Time of occurrence: night
Duration: 1 minute
Perspective: first-person defender

George was working as a locksmith, the latest in a series of odd jobs he had picked up during the lonely years since his wife had left with their young son for Texas. It was the night of January 21, 1985, during a blizzard that hit the mid-Atlantic region. George had just received a call from a woman who needed the lock to her apartment changed that night. George, always gung-ho about whatever job he lands, borrowed a friend's car and headed down to Northeast Baltimore, to the vicinity of Morgan State University (a black community college), which is in a residential neighborhood that features a drastical-

23

ly fluctuating crimescape from day to night. Strong-arm robberies and holdups are the mainstay after dark in the Northeast.

As George pulled over next to a snow bank and left his car, he realized three things: it was the coldest night of the year, it was kind of late (9:00) to be alone in this area, and he was lost. He approached two young men and asked for directions, and they offered to lead him to the apartment. George looked at the two, who resembled Rocky and Bullwinkle—one large and dark and the other smaller and light skinned—and followed as they headed up a side street.

The two stopped in the middle of the street and turned on George. "Rocky" drew a 32-caliber revolver and pressed it into George's gut, while "Bullwinkle" drew a large buck folder and held it at the ready as he quickly cleared George's front pockets with his left hand. The knife didn't concern George. He was focused on the brass casings of the shells that he could see shining under the street light as he looked down on the cylinder of the revolver that was pressed into his belly.

He was ordered to hand over his wallet. As he complied he asked, "Could I please keep the picture of my boy?"

Rocky said "No. We take it all."

Bullwinkle added, "Jus' shoot the white-mutha-fuca!"

Rocky asked, "Do you have anything else?"

George answered, "Yeah, my lock picks are on my belt."

Rocky said, "Turn around and put your hands on your head."

As George turned and was relieved of his lock picks, Bullwinkle repeated, "Jus' shoot the white muthafuca!"

Rocky then ordered, "Get down on your knees."

At this point George thought he was going to be executed, but Rocky changed his mind. "Get up and run for that [traffic] light, and don't look back."

George took off. When he got halfway to the light he still couldn't shake the thought that he would be shot in the back, so he ducked between two parked vehicles and headed for a nearby drugstore to call the police.

After making the call, he said a prayer of thanks to God for sparing his life and prayed for the souls of the robbers. When the police arrived, they seated George in the back of a cruiser and interrogated him "as if I were the criminal. They doubted my entire story and wanted to know what I was doing in this area." (It'd been a low-volume retail drug market servicing the outlying white community since the late 1970s.) George was eventually given a report number and released.

Just narrating George's story gets my vigilante blood up—where's Banno when you need him? It is my habit to try and comfort crime victims after an interview by putting their experience in context. I informed George that he was one of only two people in my study who had faced a gun and a blade at the same time—and that the other guy had been shot and stabbed.

George's ordeal was not a fight and thus, in the minds of the egotistical, arrested-development adolescents who make up the bulk of the American martial arts teaching fraternity, does not qualify as violence or as a situation worthy of self-defense study. The martial arts masters' obsession with the potential glory to be gained in ritualized, symmetrical challenges that will promote the primacy of their martial philosophy precludes the consideration of most violence in the context of their art or system.

This is the reason I wrote this book. Because most of the martial arts magazines to which I submitted knife articles could not fathom the value of studying marginal situations that do not lend themselves to cheap fight choreography. *But George was violated!*

Considering any aspect of violence—defensive firearms use, blade fighting, blunt-force attacks, group aggression—demands a broad view of aggression. Violence (and the potential for violence) results from complex human interactions and is not easily understood. Hence the religious-like practice of rigid Asian martial philosophies among squeamish, decadent Westerners. Such formalized combat models offer a convenient, easily understood mask to hang over the messy reality of human aggression.

The adoption of karate as a forum for preparing Americans to deal with personal violence reflects the need for humans to seek the comfort of delusion as much as it does our appreciation of physical artistry and the hysteria of modern fads.

Months ago, an associate of mine who is a respected traditional karate instructor and a mathematical wizard was sporting some ugly scabs on his knuckles. When I asked him about this, he replied, "I had the kids outside punching trees and Dumpsters to toughen their hands. It's bleeding now. But when it grows back it will heal stronger."

This is a perfect example of delusional thought. A man with a firm grounding in Western science, who is acting as a physical educator—and who, as a sports fan, has seen hundreds of examples of superb physical specimens losing their athletic prowess to simple repetitive-use injuries—actually believes that scar tissue is stronger than undamaged tissue! When a highly intelligent man who has access to the massive pool of sports medicine knowledge developed by his contemporaries chooses to perpetuate—indeed, inflict—rustic Asian mysticism as fact, he has chosen to seek the mirage, not the oasis.

Well, friends, I've been looking for a way out of his desert since I took my first senseless beating. . . .

ORIGINS OF THE VIOLENCE PROJECT

In 1996, a friend who had been doing calculus in school while I was warring with rival knuckle-draggers asked me to recommend a practical self-defense program. I couldn't. This led to hundreds of interviews with martial arts teachers, brawlers, criminals, and victims in an attempt to relate self-defense theory to the offensive reality of concrete burns, boot parties, brick splinters, gravel snacks, and wood shampoos.

I was not at all surprised to find a yawning abyss of ignorance separating self-defense training and the raw reality of ordinary violence in the modern United States. As the survey topped the 1,000 mark I became aware that the most common type of armed encounter was with a knife or knife-like weapon, not the firearm as the experts would have us believe. Firearm violence is the only variety of American mayhem that is not underreported. This fact, combined with my knowledge that self-defense theory regarding blade fighting is seldom presented by folks who have ever been in a real edged-weapon encounter, was the inspiration for this book.

RELATING EXPERIENCE TO SELF-DEFENSE STUDY

Since 1974, I have practiced various Western and Asian fighting arts for the purpose of self-defense. Some of these arts were taught as sports, some as meditations on the warrior tradition, and some as a means of practical combat. Regardless of their philosophical orientation, each teacher provided tools that enhanced my survivability in subsequent altercations.

Enduring beatings and surviving brawls and armed encounters had provided a context for my training. Having been taken to the pavement by a large athlete, I did not need for my wrestling coach to explain the value of the splay (sprawl). Having been sucker-punched, I did not require my boxing trainer to point out the value of rolling with a punch. When my wing chun sifu first introduced me to the art of trapping, there was no need for him to sell the point. Once you have fought in a doorway, trapping makes perfect sense. Likewise, having defended with a razor against a man wearing a leather jacket, I understood my kali instructor's emphasis on striking the hand.

Having a reference point for absorbing combat instruction is a definite advantage. The purpose of this study is to provide that advantage to those who lack real fighting experience. However, this is not just for novices. Violence is so varied that even a veteran of many altercations may lack experience in a particular area. And nobody has enough experience in real knife fights to claim expert status. Even Raphael, a veteran of perhaps a hundred acts of violence, can only recall a handful of knife encounters

DOCUMENTING VIOLENCE

My initial 21-point questionnaire proved inadequate. I eventually developed an interview technique that requires the establishment of four basic parameters:

1. Was the encounter inside or outside?
2. Did it occur at night or during the day?
3. Was the act an attack or a fight?
4. Who was the aggressor (i.e., made the first physical attempt to threaten, control, or injure)?

From here I interject enough questions during their story to satisfy six possibilities regarding the character and conduct of each party: drunk, on the job, female, acting as a group, armed, or trained. If a party is armed I get a description of the weapon and its use pattern. If the party is trained, the type of training is noted: wrestling, boxing, kickboxing, martial arts, or combatives (police fu).

Step three is result determination. Was the encounter indecisive, or was it resolved in favor of the defender or aggressor? Was either party knocked out or otherwise incapacitated because of a strike or strikes? Was there any grappling? If so, was it an upright clinch or throw, or did it go to the floor? Was the grapple resolved via knockout (KO), choke, submission, third-party intervention, or by mutual agreement or exhaustion? Did either party require medical attention (or would either have sought it if rational)? Was either arrested, charged, or sued? And did anybody die?

The perspective of the interview subjects varies from first-person defender or aggressor to eyewitness. Each perspective is deficient in some area. Eyewitnesses usually don't know if the encounter resulted in civil or criminal litigation. I personally prefer to interrogate the aggressors, especially the guys who enjoy hurting people. They are the most graphic and are most likely to recall multiple details. Crime victims offer a priceless perspective but have the most blind spots.

This study focuses on combat dynamics, so moral judgments and legal justification are not a factor in determining aggressor or

This chart is from the author's violence index. The shaded lines indicate weapon use and will (it is hoped) prevent the author from going blind compiling his statistics. Line 6 indicates use of a tool. Lines 11 and 18 indicate the use of a club. Lines 12, 17, and 19 indicate the use of a common item. Line 16 indicates the use of an edged weapon.

defender status. A police officer making an arrest is as much the aggressor as the strong-arm robber taking a wallet. Virtually none of the violence documented in this study involved law officers. Further, I am not a journalist, and only one officer consented to an interview.

I began this study with the 12 brawls and eight armed encounters in which I participated. As of this writing, I have documented 1,305 acts of violence. I use a checklist to compile the information on a graph-paper index. This permits me to generate statistics with a calculator (I have no computer).

For the blade study, I set up a separate index, copying all the relevant encounters (shaded on the main index) into four subsections: shanks, swords, razors, and knives. This should prevent me from going blind cross-indexing accounts in the main index and help preserve the cheap graph paper.

The normal course of my research nets about one blade encounter per week out of about ten. Since beginning this book I have been focusing on blades, with the effect that my overall study is becoming skewed. If I interview a veteran of 100 altercations, I will take his three knife pulls and head over to Butchers Hill in search of a knife-toting Lumbee Indian. I will eventually get back to him for the rest of his material, but until I do that with all my recent subjects, the general statistics I cite must be drawn from the initial 1,000 acts of violence. I'm no pollster, but I am trying to present a valid analysis, which must be drawn from a valid base.

CONTEMPORARY VIOLENCE TRENDS

Those interviewed for this study range from people like Raphael, whose life reads like the script of an action movie, and sociopaths like Banno to folks like Robin, a grocery clerk who survived a domestic altercation, and Scott, a historian, who, at age 11, was beaten by a group of older boys. Most of the subjects are working-class residents of Baltimore, Maryland.

- Fifty-nine percent of the action occurred outside.
- Fifty-nine percent occurred after dark.
- Sixty percent of altercations were described as an attack, instead of a voluntary fight (mutual combat).

- Fifty-three percent of violence involved alcohol or drug use.
- Seven percent of aggressors were police officers or private security personnel applying lawful force.
- Eleven percent of defenders were on the job when attacked.
- Seventeen percent of altercations actually occurred "on the street." In most cases *streetfighting* is an oxymoron.
- Twenty-five percent of violence resulted in at least one party being knocked out.
- Thirty percent of altercations ended indecisively.
- Twenty-eight percent of violence was reported to a law-officer.
- Sixteen percent resulted in an arrest, criminal charge, or civil suit.
- Sixty-three percent of violent acts were resolved in less than 10 seconds.
- Twenty-five percent of altercations lasted from 10 seconds to a minute.
- Thirteen percent lasted more than a minute.
- Three percent of female and 20 percent of male defenders were trained fighters or self-defense students.

Localized Trends

Your locale will certainly feature a unique set of violence trends, which I could only guess at —and guessing about such things is what I'm trying to avoid. I can, however, clue you in on Baltimore, in case you happen to stop by.

Northeast Baltimore is racially mixed and is the province of the lone strong-arm robber and stickup artist.

East Baltimore is home to a variety of ethnic groups: Poles, Greeks, Italians, Lumbee Indians, Central Americans, and African Americans, and is the place where you are most likely to face the lone male knifer.

South Baltimore is predominantly Caucasian and is the brawling capital of Maryland, being home to more corner bars than all other business establishments combined. Fists and blunt weapons are the rule here. Many of the folks on the South Side are descendants of immigrants from West Virginia. There is a definite Appalachian code of honor in this area.

Southwest, West, and Northwest Baltimore are predominantly African-American sections. The primary threat is made up of two young males, one of whom has a handgun. Most of the violence reported on the West Side actually represents executions and turf battles related to the drug trade. The information I have on low-profile altercations indicates the use of a lot of rocks by boys, butcher knives by men, and razors by women.

The outlying suburbs are populated by people who come from these areas and feature parallel violence trends.

THE HARD LESSONS OF AGGRESSION

The second most reliable indicator that a fighter will incapacitate an antagonist with a strike is that he or she is acting as the aggressor. Only experience in real fights counts for more.

This analysis runs contrary to my advocacy of low-intensity resolutions. When I began this study I assumed that this factor represented a male advantage, but a closer look at the numbers indicated that the higher incidence of male success in violent altercations was due to the fact that men are more likely to act as the aggressor than are women.

- Fifty-seven percent of aggressions were successful, 32 percent by KO.
- Thirteen percent of defenses were successful, 50 percent by KO.
- Thirty-two percent of aggressors were armed.
- Eight percent of defenders were armed.
- Seven percent of aggressors required medical care.
- Twenty-eight percent of defenders required medical care.
- One percent of aggressors died.
- Four percent of defenders died.
- Female aggressors were armed as often as male aggressors.
- Male defenders were five times as likely as female defenders to be armed!
- Forty-five percent of female attacks on males were successful.
- Sixty-two percent of attacks on a group by an individual succeeded.

- Seven percent of defenses by an individual against a group succeeded.

Experience is king. Aggression is queen.

INCIDENCE OF WEAPON USE
(PER 1,000 ACTS)

Weapon or Weapon Category	% of Total	% of Weapons	User Group	User Legal	INFLICTED		
					KO	Injury	Death
Blades & Shanks	11	29	23	31	19	55	12
Firearms	10	27	42	17	19	36	12
Common/Items[1]	5	13	22	10	6	18	0
Clubs (Bats)	4	10	55	16	50	71	13
Machinery[2]	2	6	27	27	41	68	14
Rocks/Trophies	2	5	55	0	30	30	5
Tools[3]	2	5	37	16	47	68	5
Sticks[3]	2	5	35	6	24	35	6
Chemical	0	0	50	0	0	50	0

NOTES

1. Bottles, shoes, etc.
2. Includes automobiles and furniture.
3. A push-broom used like a poleax is listed as a tool. If the handle is removed and wielded, it qualifies as a stick, while the broom head would qualify as a club.

- The aggressor's legal risk never exceeds the defender's risk of injury.
- Only 3 percent of armed encounters involved opposing armed parties.
- Unarmed aggressors were just as likely (+3 percent) to be victorious as were armed aggressors.

The Most Common Weapons

1. Handguns
2. Knives
3. Bottles

4. Bats
5. Razors

THE AUTHOR'S PERSPECTIVE

As a category, cutting and stabbing weapons present the most pervasive threat if you are a working-class man in Baltimore, where this survey was conducted. My information contradicts law-enforcement reports. But 72 percent of the violence I have documented went unreported, and 84 percent did not result in law-enforcement intervention or civil or criminal litigation.

Baltimore City police officers do everything possible to avoid filing a report, and the central booking system is such a joke that arrests are only made in extreme cases. The cop I talked to said that he makes people he catches with personal quantities of dope "eat it. It's their choice. If they'd rather spend three days with teenage murderers at central booking, that's their problem."

I work on the midnight shift as a grunt in a 24-hour supermarket. The employees are often called on to fight the local dope fiends who raid the store for batteries, Tylenol, deodorant, and Butterfinger bars, which they resell at bars and on buses. The cops will rarely stoop to arresting these scumballs. But they do provide us with protection from more formidable felons who might be armed with handguns.

We are lucky enough to have two really cute girls running the front end and prepared-foods departments at night, who attract a handful of cops at any given time. Having five horny cops constantly hitting on my co-workers has an additional benefit: the girls keep me informed on police activity.

A few nights ago, our Romeos in blue showed up at a stabbing in a black section of the neighborhood, but the two carved-up black dudes wouldn't talk to the cops. (Our cops love these kind of calls because there's no paperwork.) In such cases I might have one of the girls pump the cops for some additional information, but I won't inquire personally. These good ol' boys are definitely not pleased that I breathe the same air that they do. With the exception of Jason (who doubles as the front man for a thrash band), all the cops I approached were obviously put off by my curiosity—you would have thought I had INTERNAL AFFAIRS tattooed across my forehead.

Because I have personally been involved in eight edged-weapon encounters, and because knife defense is currently the province of the duelist and the deluded, I have endeavored to analyze the 200 anecdotes I've collected from my perspective: that of an experienced blade user who will probably be unarmed when next I face a knifer.

Due to the local legal climate, I no longer carry a blade and will only use a firearm for home defense. With each of my self-defense experiences, I have become more comfortable with the emergency room and less comfortable with the legal process.

THE VOICE OF LIMITED EXPERIENCE

I am not a schooled knife fighter. Nor do I train under the eye of an accredited instructor. In short, my opinion of knife use is not colored by involvement with a blade art. I have—and do—spar with wooden and rubber knives. But this is mere experimentation—valuable but not necessarily relevant to a likely blade encounter.

Like others experienced with edged-weapon use, my view is limited. In my case we are talking more breadth than depth. I am now 36 years of age, and I will relate my experience with shanks and blades to you in chronological order so that you will at least know where I am coming from.

I have variously claimed to have seven or eight such encounters, and have not completely examined my experience until this moment.

1. At age 16, I stabbed a larger punk with a pencil and snapped it off between his ribs.
2. Two months later I drove a pencil an inch deep into the thigh of a rival during an altercation on a school bus.
3. At age 18, I attempted to decapitate a very large young man with a homemade sword. He managed an outward block, and I ruined his left arm instead.
4. At age 20, I used a box cutter to defend myself against a larger man who wore a leather jacket.
5. At 26, an older man drew a razor on me, and I responded by drawing my Othello. He promptly exited stage right.

6. At age 27, I was walking to work at night on a dimly lit, tree-lined street when a Doberman pinscher attempted to pounce on me from behind. Alerted by the jangle of its choke chain, I managed to draw my utility knife just before it took the final leap. It halted and stalked away reluctantly.

7. At 32, a huge punk attempted to draw a butterfly knife on me from a belly sheath. I trapped his hand on the draw instead of going for my own blade, and this convinced me to leave the Othello at home.

8. At age 32, I warned off a punk by hitting him in the balls with the back of my blade.

9. Within a month's time I held my utility knife under the belly of a threatening drunk as we conducted our staredown. (Until I analyzed incidents 8 and 9 in light of my research, I'd never considered them as uses of the blade.)

10. At age 34, I was walking my 6-year-old boy through a school yard when we were surrounded by three young punks I'd "dissed" earlier by walking through their sinister rap session. They had followed me, and though I did not rate them a threat, they now knew how to get to my son. His school provided no security. I was compelled to establish a predatory relationship with these punks.

As my son was regaling me with a story about his second victory over an 8-year-old bully—which had played out under the watchful eye of his worthless male teacher—I stopped him and asked a question.

"Hey buddy, do you know how to kill a man with a blade?"

"No, Daddy," was his starry-eyed answer.

This development silenced the threatening punks. I then drew my blade and explained how one would kill three imaginary opponents. I concluded by reminding him that once the enemy began to spit up blood one should turn and calmly walk away. I added, "But that's my job; I just need you to stay close behind and calm. Do you understand?"

"Yes, Daddy. They're the hyenas, I'm the lion cub, and you're the daddy lion."

End of problem.

Of course, when he informed his grandmothers that Daddy was teaching him how to "kill our enemies," I had a real problem on my hands.

All this marginal experience barely amounts to one full-blown blade encounter. But these actions do give me a taste for the draw, cut, and stab (in reverse order). Although I could not rationally offer comprehensive knife fighting advice based on my own limited experience, this experience does impart an appreciation of the feeling and timing inherent in a spontaneous blade encounter.

CHAPTER 3

The Doer, the Done, and the Dumbfounded

Personal, Medical, and Legal Perspectives Under the Blade

No, no way, no charges—we
tossed the knife.

—Link Sanchez

WALKING OUT THE DOOR

Incident #42-17
Time of occurrence: night
Duration: 1 second
Perspective: first-person defender

Haynes is a former amateur boxer and tae kwon do stylist who is a musician in a cover band. He is from the South, and the type of violence and the worthless cops you run into in Baltimore just rub him the wrong way. He stands about 5 feet 10 inches and goes about 200 pounds.

One night after a gig he had a few drinks and headed out to his car. When he opened the door to the club he stepped into the middle of a "big commotion—a mess." Some jerk with a large steak or small butcher knife was stabbing at a circle of departing patrons. As Haynes shut the door behind himself, "the fool stuck me . . . right here" [indicates just below the sternum]. Haynes felt as if he had been punched. But when he lifted his shirt—while the fool lunged for someone else—he saw the hole and went to his car "to get my shit."

The knifer hadn't seen the last of Haynes, who holds a mean Southern-fried grudge. . . .

INJURY PATTERNS

Most cutting and stabbing victims will tell you that they either felt nothing or had the sensation of being punched with a fist or slapped. At least 95 percent of knife users are right-handed, with the result that most wounds are on the left side of the defender's body.

- Cuts are almost always taken on the left face, neck, and arm.
- Frontal stab wounds are often taken on the left side in the kidney and gut and up into the lung. I am, however, surprised at how many frontal stabs go to the center or perforate the liver, which is on the right side of the body.
- It appears that low cuts and stabs drift across to the target's right side, while higher strikes score on the target's extreme left. Most cuts to the leg that I am aware of were scored by right-handed knifers on the right leg of their antagonist.
- The kidney is hit as often from the front as from the back.
- Backstabbings with the overhand fell equally on the left and right shoulder of the victim.
- Backstabbings from the ready usually score below the victim's right shoulder or to one of the kidneys.
- A surprising number of cutting and stabbing victims do not seek medical attention. I do, however, classify such wounds as a medical result, because a reasonable person would seek aid.
- The most immediately debilitating injury inflicted with the blade appears to be the stab to the lung.
- The most crippling long-term stroke is the cut or stab to the opponent's hand. I know of four stabbing victims who lost the use of their right hand after the tendons were severed while attempting to grab a knifer's blade hand.

A blade held in an edge-up natural grip will be used to stab and then slice (a rip cut). This constitutes the rarest and most immediately decisive use of the blade deployed from the ready. Blades used in this manner tend to be medium-sized kitchen tools, such as fillet and carving knives.

LEGALITIES

NO PITY ON A FOOL

Incident #42-18
Time of occurrence: night
Duration: minutes
Perspective: first-person aggressor

Haynes retrieved his .38 from his car and returned to the scene of the stabbing. Although he was not willing to provide a lot of details in this incident, it appears that he backed the knifer up against the wall at gunpoint, where he administered an extensive pistol-whipping, bitch-slapping punchout. His festivities were cut short when a close friend,with his own handgun, shot the knifer in the leg.

Haynes, his friend, the knifer, and the other four stabbing victims were all hauled downtown. It appears that only the knifer and Haynes' partner did any "real time."

I am not a lawyer and do not play one on TV. I do, however, have some experience with these matters and have been advised by various lawyers. Most of the tips I'm giving you fly in the face of published legal advice and conventional wisdom. Much of my opinion about surviving the legal hassles that accompany violence is based on the experiences of fighters, criminals, and victims I have interviewed.

The following factors will contribute to your legal liability:

• Your antagonist suffered greater injury than you.
• Your antagonist was acting as a member of a group.
• You used a firearm or edged weapon.
• You are an adult male.
• Your antagonist was a minor or a female.
• Your antagonist was not armed with a firearm or blade.
• You were "winning" when the cops showed up.
• You are known to be a trained fighter or combat athlete.

All of these considerations will either put you at odds with the responding cop, stack the witness list in the other party's favor, or prejudice the judge, jury, and counsel against you.

My lawyer once told me that admitting I had been a boxer in court was legal suicide. Even if there is no case law establishing special penalties for trained fighters who use their skills in fights or self-defense situations, everyone in court will likely have the impression that you are naturally aggressive or enjoy fighting.

To get a feel for your local legal system you should simply attend some criminal court proceedings and judge for yourself. Pack a lunch. It's a hoot. As for weapons statutes, they're a local matter that you will need to check out yourself.

Here are some relevant data from my survey:

• Those who knock out their antagonist are three times more likely to face legalities.
• Those who inflict injury face criminal charges in 23 percent of cases, in contrast to the 16-percent average.
• Those who kill face criminal charges in 48 percent of incidents.

(This reflects the fact that only one member of a group that beats a man to death will actually be charged with a crime. The guys who hold you down while the primary aggressor kicks you in the head will end up in court as witnesses, for him or the state.)

- Three percent of groups who fought or attacked individuals had all of the members arrested or charged.
- Three percent of individuals attacked by groups faced criminal charges.

Minimizing Legal Liabilities against the Knifer

If you have a reliable witness—preferably a loyal woman—you can pound an opponent into the pavement and probably beat any charges. (Remember, whoever gets hurt the worst is the good guy in the eyes of the law.)

If your opponent has an accomplice, I suggest that you drag him into the fight and mark him up. If he's not bruised or bloodied, the knifer's sidekick will miraculously become an innocent bystander who happened to see you "jump the little guy from behind"—and if the cops don't buy it, the court commissioner or flunky assistant state's attorney will. And you can bet your bank account that the ambulance chaser who advertises on local late-night TV will lick it up!

In most cases you and the knifer will be alone for up to 10 seconds. By then you're either fajita steak or you're looking like the bad guy to whoever passes by, so you should probably opt for a restraining hold—and some hideous threats whispered into his ear while you wait for the cops to show.

Don't pick up the knife unless it's you, him, and an alley full of rodents, or you might find out how the big boyz perforate lungs in the state pen. Use of a blade results in a high ratio of legal action.

The stats in the table on page 44 were derived by dividing the legal risk associated with using a certain weapon type by the incidence of injuries inflicted with that weapon type.

Example: Knifers face criminal charges in 31 percent of altercations and inflict injury in 55 percent of altercations, indicating that 56 percent (at most) of injurious blade use puts the knifer in legal jeopardy.

WEAPON	LEGALITY-INJURY RATIO (PERCENTAGES)
Blade	56
Common items	55[1]
Firearm	47
Machinery	29
Tools	24
Bats/Clubs	23
Sticks	17
Rocks/Bricks, etc.	0!

NOTE

1. This reflects more the ineffectiveness of such weapons than the legal liability associated with their use.

Note that the injurious use of a weapon rarely carries more than a 50 percent chance of legal action. The armed aggressor's overall legal risk *never* exceeds the defender's risk of injury.

Think twice about turning an attacker's blade against him. As for using your own blade, cops *hate* knives; most of the folks on your jury couldn't stomach cutting their own steak, and your lawyer will think you are an idiot or crazy.

As the above table demonstrates, the blade is the most taboo weapon in today's United States.

KNIFER AS VILLIAN

In civilized societies the knife has always been the mark of the underclass. During the colonial period in North America, the knife was also the mark of the "subhuman" aborigine, who was usually able to best his civilized oppressor in close combat. With the Industrial Revolution, killing calmly at a distance replaced the "savage" close-in fight as the favored combat model. Knives are just too personal for most people.

In modern times, fear and hatred of the knife have been inculcated into the police officer, who is taught that he will not be able to draw his firearm on a knife-armed felon who is within 20 feet without first being stabbed by such a fiend. When you take a blade in your hand, you become the arch enemy of every cop in the United States.

This has resulted in some unfortunate overreactions by police, one of which I saw on videotape—involving the shooting of a pathetic, disoriented boy who was showing the blade to cops who already had their guns drawn. The kid was freezing before their eyes, but they couldn't let it go. Lucky for me it was a black cop who did the shooting otherwise I might have been dragged off the bus that very day.

Now, killing with a blade is gruesome, and many knifers are certainly cowardly and villainous. So, if you choose to use a blade, keep in mind that those who hate you for it have some justification, as the following altercations show.

SAVING FACE

Incident #26-10:
Time of occurrence: night
Duration: minutes
Perspective: eyewitness

Big John and Little Tony got into a street-corner fight for no good reason. Little Tony proceeded to "beat the piss outta" Big John, in what turned out to be an extended, one-sided fistfight. Eventually a friend put a sheath knife into John's right hand, which he used to slash the left side of Tony's neck.

Tony didn't notice the cut and continued to fight with blood streaming from his neck. John panicked at the sight of Tony's massive blood loss and ran.

John and his accomplice were arrested, charged, and convicted, getting between one and three years. Tony survived the near-fatal wound.

There is a lesson to be learned here about depending on the shock of even a heavy blade's strike. If it's not heavy enough to club with the back or flat effectively expect it to fail as a shock weapon. And if it's razor sharp that will lessen the sensation of being cut even more. When used defensively, I recommend showing the blade after you score, just so your opponent knows what's happening to him. That is the best way to shock with a knife.

In regard to using or defending against the blade, if you are reasonably athletic and aggressive and have a fair amount of fighting skill, you will realize how easy it is to cut a man the moment you feel a blade in your hand.

When and where is all this cutting and stabbing going on?

INCIDENTS OF KNIFE USE BY LOCALE
(PERCENTAGES)

WEAPON TYPE			LOCALE		
	Surface	Walkway	Lot/yard	Indoors	Natural setting
Razor	13	36	10	38	3
Shank	7	7	7	75	4
Knife	7	34	14	40	5
Sword	8	16	-	75	-

INCIDENCES OF KNIFE USE BY TIME
(PERCENTAGES)

Weapon	Night	Day
Razor	56	44
Shank	37	63
Knife	63	37
Sword	83	17

CHAPTER 4

Twerps, Goons, and Bloodthristy Babes

Profiles of the Knife-Armed Antagonist

There's a lot of people out there now that will put a bullet in your back or get somebody after you. But he was hard-core; he would bring it to you.

—Jason

THE TRAINED KILLER NEXT DOOR

Incident #27-01 & 27-02
Time of occurrence: night
Duration: 1–3 seconds each
Perspective: a reliable secondhand source who witnessed a portion of the action

In the early autumn of 1984, Billy and his brothers held an end-of-summer party at the oldest brother's ranch house. Like most ranch homes in the suburbs of Pittsburgh, this one was cut into the top of a hill, with a driveway in the front and a backyard sloping down to a thick stand of woods.

People arrived throughout the afternoon, parking in the neighbor's yard and playing loud music. All of this aggravated John, the next-door neighbor. A former Navy SEAL and Vietnam combat veteran in his late 30s, John was 6 feet tall, weighed over 200 pounds, and was a little out of shape.

Billy, a 20-year-old wrestler and football player, was the same height and weight as John. After arguing with John about the parking arrangements and loud music more than once, Billy noticed that some of the car tires had been slashed. He confronted John, and a heated argument ensued, which resulted in Billy's knocking out John with a sucker punch. Billy and his brother returned to the party, leaving John lying unconscious in his yard.

Some time later, after dark, Billy, his brothers, and a few girls were drinking beer on the back deck, which was built rather close to the ground. Billy was leaning on the railing on his left side, having a conversation with someone to his left. No one recalled seeing John walk up the side stair behind Billy's right. He just seemed to materialize with a knife in his hand.

John plunged the blade (it is unclear whether this was a sheath or folding knife) down into Billy's right trapezius, slicing down across the shoulder blade to the right, through the midportion of the latissimus dorsi, and out to the side. Billy described feeling "a hard burning sensation" as if he had been electrocuted.

As Billy leaned forward and began to turn right, John plunged the blade into his side, driving it up under the last rib and collapsing the right lung. Billy finished his turn, reached out for John, but folded onto the deck.

John took off into the woods and didn't reappear for a couple of days, but he was eventually arrested and charged with assault. While waiting for his court date, John was physically assaulted and harassed repeatedly by Billy's brothers. John eventually beat the rap on a mental incapacity plea and moved away.

Billy lost mobility in his right arm and had to stop playing football. He has since regained use of the arm through physical therapy.

I counted John's attack as a slice and a stab from the overhand.

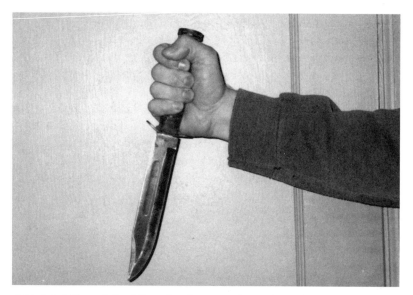

A blade held in an "edge in" overhand grip may be used to stab and slice (rip cut). The only cuts known to have been inflicted from a blade or shank used from the overhand posture were downward pressure cuts, one inflicted with a large tactical blade and another with an ice pick.

THE SERIOUS KNIFER

The above encounter is atypical in that it involved a knifer who had been trained in the use of his weapon. Besides there aren't enough former Navy SEALs running around to constitute a statistically significant risk—even if they are inclined to take out your tires and your lung.

The serious knifer is not a deluded punk brandishing his blade

for ego projection. Nor is he the paralyzed attacker depicted in martial arts demonstrations, advancing flat-footed with a lead-hand
lunge or an overhand ice-pick plunge.

There are knife carriers who are incapable of employing their
weapon effectively, which is often a mental crutch. However, using
such a weak opponent as the focus for your self-defense training is
also a crutch that only builds false confidence.

The serious knifer does not show the blade unless he has a practical reason to do so, like terrifying a woman, or warning off a man.
The man or woman who uses a blade is expressing a practical or
emotional need for an edge: an advantage.

Humans are tool-using predators. It's what we've been about
since the dawn of time, and using weapons is a tendency that's likely to stay with us. Your most likely knife-armed adversary is a real
person, with all-too-real feelings, who is seeking a lethal advantage
over you, either in premeditation or in response to a heated situation.

The type of blade-armed aggressors worthy of your training
focus are the following:

1. Trained knifer
2. Prison knifer
3. Advantage knifer (effective but untrained)

The Trained Knifer
The most likely attackers are not former government-trained
killers or martial artists trained in the Filipino blade arts. Only 1 percent of knife-armed aggressors are—or appear to be—schooled in
the use of the blade (compared to 2 percent of weapon users overall).
The opportunistic criminal or vicious alcoholic does not possess the
self-discipline to pursue an art to potential. Escrimidors are not
inclined to rob, rape, or murder fellow citizens.

The Prison Knifer
The prison knifer—being a compulsive killer—is the most dangerous knifer. But he spends much of his life behind bars and when
released is just as likely to use a handgun as a knife. He is not a likely knife-armed assailant outside the joint.

The Advantage Knifer

The advantage knifer, while not as dangerous as the trained or prison types, is the most common blade user. He is the subject of this profile. The following incidents exemplify the knife user whose primary reason for carrying a blade is to stay off the bottom of the food chain.

RICK WAYNE

Incident #10-04
Time of occurrence: day
Duration: 10–20 seconds
Perspective: first-person aggressor

"This was in Atlantic City, back in '87 or '88, when I was juiced [body building]. My buddy and I were cruisin' down Pacific Avenue in the Land Cruiser when this guy ran in front of my vehicle— in my path! I got mad because I almost hit him and got out and chased him.

"I chased this guy up against a fence and started yelling at him. His friend is yelling that he was drunk. My hearing was getting fuzzy I was so mad. So I couldn't make out what else he said. Two skinny Spanish guys drinking.

"While I was yelling at this guy, my friend was yelling, 'He's got a knife!'—meaning the guy's friend. But I never saw it. His right side was turned to me, and he must've been left-handed. When I realized the guy was drunk, I got back into the Land Cruiser—it was in the middle of the street. When I got in Kevin was saying, 'Didn't you realize he had a knife?' He was panicked because he couldn't figure out how to work the latch."

This is a rare example of someone's effectively holding a weapon at the ready without showing it. In such cases, the knife is usually only noticed by third parties. But it does give the knifer the confidence to pursue a verbal solution with an antagonist.

Of course, sometimes the twerp is not showing, concealing, or striking with the weapon. . . .

HARRY THE GOOF

Incident #48-11 & 48-12
Time of occurrence: night
Duration: 15 seconds
Perspective: first-person aggressor

While tending bar at his establishment, Tattoo Rick was trying to ignore a runt called Harry the Goof. When Death Metal Ron, "a big freak," left to use the men's room, Harry started talking with Ron's girl. When he returned, Ron was quite miffed at this turn of events and asked Rick, "What the fuck is a matter with this guy?"

Rick—in his inimitable style—said, "Kill him."

As Ron began to crowd Harry—a man twice his age and half his size—Rick went into his "see no evil" mode, busying himself behind the bar. Seconds later Ron said, "Rick, look."

Rick looked over and saw that Harry had deployed a Buck folder.

"He had his left side to the bar, his back to me, and was holding it down at his right side, not waving it around. I thought that was kind of ominous," Rick recalled.

As Ron and Harry continued their standoff, Rick, a large former kickboxer, walked around the bar, came up on Harry's right side, and did a simultaneous downward biceps/rising forearm slap, which ejected the blade over Harry's shoulder. Rick then did a sweeping throw, which sent Harry to the floor. When Harry began to rise, Rick side-kicked

him in the chest, sending him into the bar, followed
by a rear-leg round kick that drove Harry's head
back into the bar face.
Ron was relieved, the patrons were entertained,
and Rick was very pleased with his side kick.
However, Rick is never pleased about having to drag
a body 50 feet away from his bar. He has a bad back
and claims that "loser removal" is the most hazardous
aspect of bouncing. Good thing Harry was a runt.

There are three types of advantage knifers out there. They are,
from most to least common:

1. Twerps, little guys who need a knife
2. Goons, monstrous sociopaths like Banno, who just like to make
   sure you get the point
3. Bloodthirsty babes bent on homicide

The Twerp

The person who uses a knife to gain a tactical advantage is usually
a small male or at least smaller than his antagonist. Because the blade
is a weapon the requires little leverage and any part of the defender's
anatomy is vital under the blade (most major arteries are within an inch
of the skin), the big man is at a serious disadvantage.

The typical twerp is not a success story. Usually unemployed, he
is addicted to hard drugs and suffers from alcohol-induced sexual
dysfunction. Working at menial jobs colors his perception of incar-
ceration: for him a prison sentence is not the potential horror that it
is for you. He is unhappy and believes he has little to lose.

The twerp is almost certainly a pedestrian. Not being tied to an
identifiable asset (car) makes him hard to arrest. He is also in fair to
good physical condition, especially his legs.

He may have used an edged tool as a condition of employment
(during those infrequent periods) as a seafood or stock clerk, meat
cutter, or carpet layer. Such experience is relevant. He is also accus-
tomed to redirecting his fears or doubts (concerning the law or a victim) into controlled rage.

Background

Your typical knife-wielding twerp is an experienced—though not dominant—fighter. Marginal results in brawls may have led him to adopt the blade as an extension of himself. (This is the proper blade fighting attitude.) In any case, he has two live hands, will not panic when hit, and is still a threat without the knife.

He has little or no formal training. His skills have been developed by stabbing schoolmates with pencils or pens, killing small animals, playing chicken with folding knives (and hence being cut), and stick fighting as a teen. His most highly developed skill is deploying the blade from a concealed position. This is something he practices daily, more often than a typical martial artist practices attack responses.

He may have done time in jail or prison and has almost certainly been housed in a juvenile detention facility. Regardless of his record, his associates include felons who have committed violent crimes. His appreciation of the knife is based largely on the experiences of older thugs.

Choice of Weapon

His weapon will most likely be a folding blade of some type: lock blade, penknife, balisong, or switchblade, with a 3- to 5-inch blade. This is the kind of guy who carries a weapon, as opposed to picking up what is lying around.

GOING TO THE DANCE

Incident #44-03
Time of occurrence: night
Duration: 1 second
Perspective: eyewitness

Ben and Phillip, two average black dudes growing up in the 1960s, were headed to a dance at a school in Turner Station, an old black waterfront community on the outskirts of Dundalk, Maryland, which is an eastern suburb of Baltimore. As they stepped off the bus, Ben was ahead and to the right of Phillip when suddenly Phillip lurched forward, falling face first onto the walk.

The handle of "a good-sized Buck folding knife" was sticking out of his left lower back. The boy who had obviously put the knife in Phillip's kidney was already running off into the night.

Phillip was seriously incapacitated. According to the ambulance crew who arrived within 20 minutes, he would have died had the knife not been left in the wound. The two white county cops who showed up at the scene made no inquires about the identity of the knifer and filed the incident as "gang related" (black on black). The motive or identity of the knifer was never made clear to Ben. Phillip recovered and has led an ordinary life since then.

Goons and Sociopaths

BULL

Incident #44-13
Time of occurrence: night
Duration: 10–15 seconds
Perspective: eyewitness

Bull was a big, mean, crazy drunk who liked to fight—and could—but absolutely hated to lose. One night, he came into Duke's club in Texas and picked a fight with two smaller guys, one of whom turned out to be pretty tough.

"Bull was doin' all right, but things didn't go juss so, so he cut one a the boys—a cross-cut to the gut—en run. He knew I'd buss a cap in 'is ass. I done told him so the firs' time he whipped that thang out. That one big, crazy muthafuca."

Bloodthirsty Babes

Over the course of my first 600 acts of violence I didn't come across a single example of a woman using a knife—razors, yes; knives, no. Then I started surveying Baltimore's South Side. So much for my original theory that knives are some sort of phallic symbol that keeps women at bay. I'm sure Odysseus would be able to handle these women, but the boys from the city's Northeast wouldn't stand a chance.

IN THE KITCHEN

Incident #21-16
Time of occurrence: night
Duration: 2 seconds
Perspective: Rickey, first-person defender

"Yeah. At night. Always at night, inside, and drinkin'. My wife was cookin' on the stove and talkin' on the phone, while my daughter and I were arguing. She's a teenager, you know, like that. Back-talker.

"Well, I smacked her. Been drinkin'. That's the way it goes, drinkin'. My wife turned from the stove with the butcher knife she was using in the pan and ran it behind my shoulder blade. It came out under the arm. I didn't feel the blade. But I knew it when she hit me over the head with the phone.

"I waited three days before I went to the emergency room. I'd been drinkin'. There was a pocket of this dark blood they drained from under my arm. It turned out OK. I got hurt worse twistin' my ankle on the curb out front fightin' that guy couple months back.

"We divorced again. I ain't goin' back this time. I'm tired of fightin' all the time. I want a woman to love, not fight."

Ricky's got a new girl, and he doesn't fight the cops any more either. They killed his brother. He doesn't want any of that.

BLEEDING ON SUE'S STOOP

Incident #38-07
Time of occurrence: night
Duration: 5 seconds
Perspective: eyewitness

Sue, a medical transcriber, likes to lie across her bed with the window open on a warm night. One summer night as she was enjoying the night air, her peace and quiet were interrupted by a domestic squabble between two men and a woman. The woman was armed with a butcher knife.

As the man who appeared to be the husband or boyfriend backed toward Sue's front door, the woman brought the blade up from her right side and lunged at him, running the point through the center of his belly.

As the woman and the other man fled, Sue ran downstairs to render first aid. When she tried to open her storm door, she noticed to her horror that the seriously injured man was lying on her top step and blocking her door. She was afraid to push too hard for fear that she would tumble the injured man down the steps. She settled for calling 911.

The man lived, the woman who knifed him was arrested, and Sue eventually got the stains off her stairs.

TRAVESTIES WITH THE BLADE

The following knifers could actually be defeated by the otherwise suicidal antiknife techniques promoted by the self-proclaimed martial arts masters who stride pompously across the pages of martial arts magazines.

I, HAVE, A, KNIFE.

Incident: #47-09
Time of occurrence: day
Duration: 2 seconds
Perspective: first-person defender

Bryant, a successful kickboxer and streetfighter, was approached by a high school rival in a hallway between classes. His rival produced a knife, held it rigidly at arm's length between himself and Bryant, and froze. Bryant disarmed him with a reverse crescent kick and continued on his way, as the wimp ran back down the hall, leaving his blade on the floor.

MANNY THE MAN

Incident #51-09
Time of occurrence: night
Duration: 30–60 seconds
Perspective: first-person defender

"It was a few years back in the middle of January on North Avenue, where they used to have the Geno's. Tone and I were minding our own drunken business when this black kid—couldn't have been more than 14 years old—comes up to us, pulls out this steak knife or a similar sort of cheesy blade and demands our money.

"He showed it to us and held it right here [in front of right hip] and the fuckin' kid thinks he's goin' to get our money.

"I said, 'Yeah, sure, here it is,' and put my .38 in his face.

"Tone pulls out this cheap, small-caliber piece-of-junk—something worthless—and the kid's in shock. We robbed him. Took his money, knife, jacket, shoes, and socks. He was crying while he peeled off his socks. It was a cold night."

Manny is a large, bald tattoo artist, who is the only subject in my survey who has successfully used a jug full of urine as a weapon.

It is becoming quite obvious to me that an aggressor who shows a blade from the lead is either demonstrating gross incompetence or lacking the aggressive nature necessary to employ such a close-range weapon effectively.

And, for our crowning travesty of blade use, I present Joel the Drunk. . . .

DON'T MOVE!

Incident #41-04
Time of occurrence: night
Duration: 7–9 seconds
Perspective: first-person defender

Mike, a 6-foot, 8-inch Goth, was drinking at a bar for the first time in his life. He was only 19, but the owner served him on occasion. On a barstool to his right was Joel, a potbellied runt in his 30s, who had been hassling him over something entirely forgettable. Joel grabbed Mike's right arm, so Mike swept the stool away with his right foot, and Joel sprawled backward onto the floor.

As he sat up, Joel drew a sheath knife from his back pocket. Even though he was towering over Joel, Mike had to admit, "It certainly was a surprise. I have no idea how he concealed the thing."

As soon as Joel brought the blade out to his right side he made an inward cut from his seated position on the floor, catching Mike across the right shin. As Joel either made a pathetic attempt to rise or strike again (it's not clear which) Mike—whose back was to the bar—reached down, grabbed him by the upper sleeves, and threw him against the bar. The knife clattered to the floor.

Mike kept Joel pinned to the bar with his left hand as he picked up the knife with his right. He happened to pick it up in an ice-pick grip, and since Joel "was trying to squirm away from the bar," he decided to put the blade to good use. Mike pinned Joel's right wrist to the bar with his left hand and drove the blade through the back of Joel's hand. The blade "thunked into the bar top," effectively pinning Joel's hand to the bar.

Mike turned and ran out into the night, which is where he likes it.

Note that Joel, fool though he was, did not miss with his ill-conceived inward stroke.

CHAPTER 5

Shaving Sideways

The Use of Razors

It needs to be realized that fighting tactics come from techniques, and techniques are derived primarily (though not exclusively) from the mechanics of the weapon itself.

—John Clements
Renaissance Swordsmanship

The above maxim most definitely applies to razor fighting. As you will see, fighting with a razor is a messy proposition and is not a recommended means of self-defense. Knives, shanks, and especially razors are most effective as stealth weapons. Of all blades, razors are the most likely to be used during a fight by a losing party desperate for an edge.

All razors are unreliable impact weapons and require the user to work within grappling range. Coats, jackets, and any double layers of clothing offer a high degree of protection against these weapons. Unless you are bare-chested or wearing a light T-shirt, the razor user will go for the face, neck, or thigh.

The variety of razor tools suitable for stealth attacks available for under $2 is astounding.

THE BOX CUTTER

The box cutter is a simple, easily concealed weapon that can be quickly deployed. Its weakness is the tendency of the blade to break

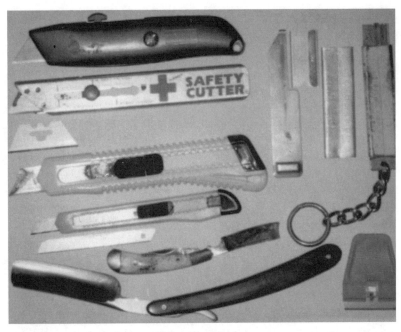

An assortment of razors, razor tools, and utility knives.

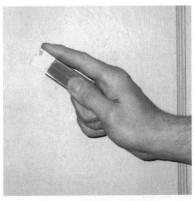

The slicing grip, used in the grapple, is usually deployed from the front pants pocket.

The slashing grip, usually deployed from the rear pocket, is used for an inward cut.

on impact with wood, metal, or bone. The maximum depth of cuts inflicted is 1/2 inch.

A reliable blind draw (that faces the blade edge away from the user's hand) is facilitated by loading the blade holder into the slide so that the crease of the slide faces away from the palm and can be felt with the thumb. When deployed from the rear pocket, the blade is exposed by tapping the back of the holder against the thigh or hip.

Draws from the front pocket need to be quicker. Therefore, the blade is exposed by pushing the butt of the holder forward with the pinkie finger or heel of the hand while the hand is still in the pocket.

In all cases, the box cutter is most reliable when the holder is stabilized in a forward position by palming the butt. The blade is only sharp when unused and is more likely to snap when nicked or dull. As a last-ditch defensive weapon, the box cutter should be pocketed with a fresh blade.

For defensive purposes the recommended target is a thigh. This will help avoid maiming charges and disfigurement suits. The thigh is easy to hit from the low pocket draw and will produce a lot of blood. In case you don't like the idea of your antagonist bleeding all over you, keep in mind that bleeding the opponent is what combative razor use is all about.

EARNING TIME SERVED

Incident #18-25
Time of occurrence: night
Duration: 20–40 seconds
Perspective: first-person defender

Spider, a large ponderous grocery clerk, was out at a local club with his old lady, a very stout woman. Spider allowed himself to get involved in a confrontation with a larger, more aggressive man. The man knocked Spider to the floor, mounted him, and began dishing out the right hands.

Spider's old lady tried to pull the goon off but was unsuccessful. The goon eventually became irritated with her cramping his punching style. Without giving up the mount, he made a half-turn, grabbed the 250-pound woman by her belt, and tossed her across the room.

This was too much for Spider, who had just managed to draw his case cutter from his front pocket. When the goon tossed his old lady he had shifted his grip from Spider's right shoulder sleeve to his collar, freeing Spider's right arm. The goon was still looking half over his right shoulder in the direction of the sprawled woman when Spider brought the blade up and sliced open the left side of his attacker's neck from ear to throat. As the goon lurched to the side in shock, Spider was restrained by security. Spider was jailed for some weeks while awaiting trial. Thanks to the testimony of his old lady and the record of the goon, the judge sentenced Spider to time already served.

UTILITY KNIVES

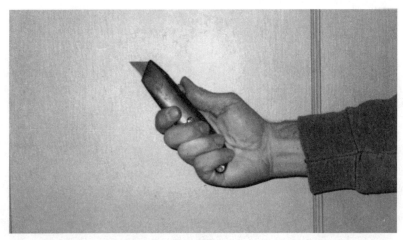

The standard utility knife. The thumb placement necessary to push the blade out is the weak link during deployment. If your aim is to control your opponent's weapon hand or disarm him, act before he gets a natural grip on the knife.

DIDLISH

Incident #51-02
Time of occurrence: day
Duration: 56 seconds
Perspective: eyewitness

"It was in '76, probably April because we were all still wearing jackets. We were outside the school, about 7:00 in the morning, hanging out, getting high. This was at Herring Run Junior High. I was 13, and I'll never forget that morning.

"These two older kids came up and the front guy asked for Didlish, who was a moocher, a real dirtbag who never bought his own weed. Somebody pointed him out, and the older kid walked up and punched him in the face.

"Didlish kind of crumpled up and reached into the top left pocket of his denim jacket and pulls out this case knife. He stands up and starts waving the thing around like this [demonstrates a move from *West Side Story*] while the older kids took off their belts. The one kid was standing back looking at us like, 'You all want any of this?'

"The first kid had this huge belt buckle—don't know what kind it was. But he swung it over his head and clocked Didlish right on the forehead. Knocked him out cold. Then he pointed his finger and said, 'That'll teach you to steal my little brother's bike!' and walked away. It was poetic justice. Didlish was nothin' but a petty common thief."

STRAIGHT RAZORS

I used to know a guy up Wess Bolmore who use a straight razor, en he get rid of it so the cops couldn't find it—he neva got in trouble.

—Duke

With the exception of black women, the straight razor seems to have fallen into disuse as a weapon. Almost every incident I have documented happened before 1990. This may be related to the high cost and low availability of the traditional razor when compared to cheap razor tools.

For those interested in the defensive application of the straight razor, I recommend reading *Close Shaves* by Bradley J. Steiner (available from Loompanics Unlimited).

HIGH NOON IN THE JANITOR'S ROOM

Incident #48-09
Time of occurrence: day
Duration: 10–20 seconds
Perspective:

Mouse was 15 and the new kid in a rural high school. This was in the 1960s, and his long hair and hippie style didn't sit well with the local farmboys.

On his third day in school someone had taken his pencil and broken it into pieces, which they threw at the back of his head while he sat in class. He got up and stalked to the back of the room where "our fuckin' hillbillies" were seated and asked, "Which one of you took my pencil?"

"Naturally, it was the biggest, meanest-lookin' mutherfucker in the room, Sam McNutt, a big dude, a football player. They called me Hair Tree. I was very small, and, of course, the girls were all into the hippie thing. Needless to say, these big, dumb farm-boys weren't too happy with that.

"We agreed to meet in the janitor's room the next day. Lunchtime I think. Time to put on your ass-kicking pants. The other pants were the lookin' cool up-your-ass type for the girls—hip-huggers. These pants were still cool but old.

"I walk into the janitor's room, and there's six

guys lined up against the wall, and I figure this guy is going to kill me. He says, 'I'll give you the first punch.' So I kicked him in the balls. All it did was piss him off.

"I could box pretty well. My uncle had trained me, and I won my fights at the Y. I was jabbin' this guy—trying to roll with the punches—but he was killing me. He was really knocking me around. He actually pushed me down with a spent punch.

"Well, I said, 'Fuck this!' and went for my razor. I kept it in the back pants pocket. There really aren't many practical carry options with blades. You try putting it in the boot or sock or whatever, and you're either on the ground or your foot's up your ass getting it out.

"So I get this thing out—brandish it—take a swipe, and say, 'Come on!' Well, this guy—he wasn't a bad guy, honorable and everything—he was pretty well convinced that I'd do it. It was like, 'OK, everybody, time to go.' Those guys never gave me any trouble after that."

RAZOR BLADES

The use of loose razor blades is rare and certainly endangers the user. This is as messy as it gets and makes for some colorful situations.

SLAP AND SLASH

Incident #44-12
Time of occurrence: night
Duration: 20–30 seconds
Perspective: eyewitness

A bouncer in a Texas nightclub was waiting for his cue to intervene as two large black dudes were slapping a small Mexican around. "They were laughing, and the Mexican was laughing." And then there was some blood.

The Mexican was slapping the guy to his front and laughing merrily as the two bouncers now looked on and tried to figure out what was going on. "It appeared that the Mexican had a broken nose, so it was time to step in."

When the bouncers got close the Mexican was laughing hysterically as he was being slapped in the head and face with great force, from front and back. At this point, the bouncers could see that the black man facing the Mexican, and who was also laughing, had a great stream of blood flowing from a half-dozen cuts to his neck.

When the three were restrained, the bouncers found a razor between the Mexican's fingers. All three of the slappers were arrested and jailed.

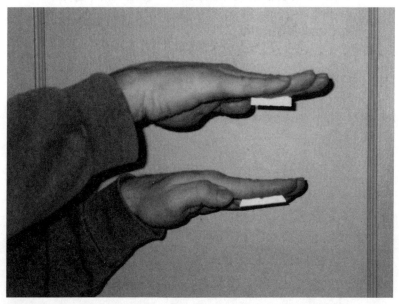

The Mexican slapper with standard razor (top) and utility razor (bottom).

UNDER THE BRIDGE

Incident #29-07
Time of occurrence: day
Duration: seconds
Perspective: first-person defender

Jacob, a kind man in his late 60s, saw what appeared to be an unconscious young man sprawled under a bridge in the crime-ridden black section of East Baltimore, not far from the famous Johns Hopkins Hospital. When he leaned over to help, the young man jumped up, cut him on the left hand and over the left eye with a razor blade, and stole his wallet.

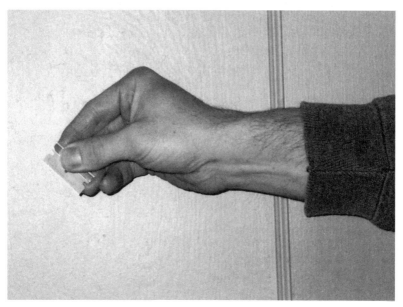

The urban American slicer is the last-ditch edged weapon of the prowling dope fiend.

AT THE BUS STOP

Incident #50-11
Time of occurrence: day
Duration: 10–15 seconds
Perspective: eyewitness

George was standing at the bus stop after school in a rough section of Northeast Baltimore, when he noticed a black boy threatening a schoolmate. The black boy began kicking the white kid in the leg. After three kicks with the heel of his shoe, the white kid submitted and "listened to whatever the other boy had to say."

George could see that the khaki pants of the victim were streaked with blood below the left knee. He also noticed that the black boy plucked something out of the heel of his right shoe before walking off. He later learned that a razor blade had been embedded into a slot cut into the heel and that this was common practice among black boys in that part of town in the 1950s.

The Unseen Blade

I have documented a handful of attacks in which the defender suffered deep, fine cuts that appeared to be inflicted by a razor of some kind, even though there was no other evidence that the attacker was armed. Below is a case in point.

CLOSING TIME

Incident #47-11
Time of occurrence: night
Duration: 10–15 seconds
Perspective: eyewitness

Raphael, who works as a bouncer and a medical

technician, was working at a club on U.S. Route 40, when two black chicks "got into an argument over some unknown issue." It was 2:00 A.M., and before Raphael and his boys could clear the club he heard a crash of glass as the right-most woman swept her right hand across the bar top and into the other girl. At this point, both women tumbled from their barstools and began wrestling on the floor amid the broken bottles and glasses that had tumbled off the bar.

Within seconds Raphael had separated the two, throwing the aggressor to one of his boys and restraining the defender, who began fighting him. He thrust his pen light into her sternum to knock her back and then noticed that the inside of her thigh had been laid open to the bone. It was a clean 12-inch cut from knee to groin, which exposed the femoral artery and, in his opinion, was too long, deep, and clean to have been caused by the girl's rolling in glass or even by a deliberate stroke with a shard of glass or broken bottle.

As Raphael attempted to render first aid he was attacked by the girl's boyfriend, whom he KO'd with a double-palm thrust to the chest. As he returned to the girl, who was going into shock, a friend of the boyfriend tried to blind-side him but was bear-hugged and thrown into a wall by Dante, Raphael's largest fellow bouncer.

Raphael improvised a bandage and attempted to call 911, but was blocked by the club manager who didn't want any cops showing up at his establish-ment. The girl and the fools who'd brought her were sent down the road to the nearest hospital.

Raphael and I reenacted the incident in his living room. This was not difficult: he had witnessed the entire event as he had made his way across the floor of the establishment. His ability to focus under physical stress is amazing. By combining my research on edged-weapon use with his experience in the medical field, we came to the conclusion that the aggressor in this incident most likely had used a straight razor.

• • •

I began this chapter by noting that razors are unreliable impact weapons, which I do not recommend for self-defense. I favor impact weapons because I am small and do not like to grapple. I must admit that the razor may be the most effective weapon in the grapple.

Consider Spider's fight with the goon. That goon was prevailing easily against 500+ pounds of determined monogamy. But one slice of the cheapest razor blade that money can buy took him out of the fight. The razor is a weapon to be reckoned with.

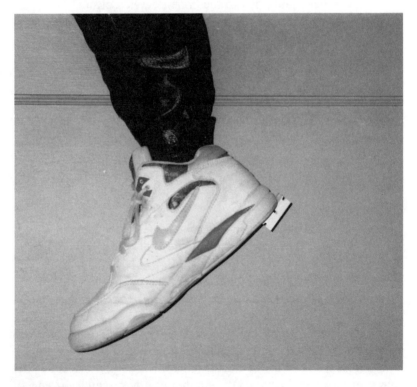

The heel-mounted razor blade.

40 ACTS OF RAZOR USE

	TECHNIQUES						POSTURES		
Weapon	% Use	Hold	Show	Warn	Slash	Slice	Lead	Ready	Overhand
Cutter	30	-	25	-	33	42	58	42	-
Utility	23	11	67	11	11	-67	22	11	
Straight	27	-	9	9	36	46	18	82	-
Loose	13	-	-	-	60	40	20	80	-
Unseen	2	-	-	-	-	100	-	100	-
Glass	5	-	50	-	50	-	50	50	-

	ARMED AGGRESSOR					ANTAGONIST				
Weapon	Group	KO'd	Med.	Leg.	Dth.	Armed	KO'd	Med.	Leg.	Dth.
Cutter	10	-	-	40	-	20	-	70	-	-
Utility	50	-	-	-	-	-	-	50	-	-
Straight	-	-	-	67	-	-	11	89	-	11
Loose	25	-	-	25	-	-	-	100	-	-
Unseen	-	-	-	-	-	-	-	100	-	-
Glass	-	-	100	50	-	-	-	100	50	-

	ARMED DEFENDER					ANTAGONIST				
Weapon	Group	KO'd	Med.	Leg.	Dth.	Armed	KO'd	Med.	Leg.	Dth.
Cutter	50	-	50	50	-	50	-	50	-	-
Utility	-	14	-	-	-	14	-	-	-	-
Straight	-	-	-	50	-	-	-	100	50	-
Loose	-	-	100	100	-	-	-	100	100	-

CHAPTER 6

Getting Boned

The Use of Various Knives

I don't mess with nothin but top a da line stuff when it comes to my life. So when I stuck 'um with that Barlow he scream like a stuck pig. Over a hundred stitches the cop said. Every time he take a bath he muss think a me. Neva take pity on a fool, neva know what he might do. Count three buttons down.

—Haynes

Whatever you might think of Hayne's choice of blade, he certainly knows how to use it, and he at least considers the quality of his weapon as a factor. Most knifers will settle for complete junk. The lock blade that Haynes wielded for his demonstration (right next to the corn-on-the-cob display at the market where I work and he shops) was a worn barlow folder with a wide 5 1/2-inch blade. I think it was the same one he used on the above fool.

I AIN'T NO WHITEBOY!

Incident #43-13
Time of occurrence: night
Duration: minutes
Perspective: first person

Haynes and the boys in the band had just finished a gig on the West Side, and he had been detailed to buy the liquor. He stepped into a place called Token's Bar, broke a big bill out of his money

roll (he always carries a big wad of dough in a pocket next to one of his blades), and made a purchase.

Token's was one of those booze stands common
in the poorer black sections of town. There are no
windows that haven't been barred, boarded, or bar-
raged with posters, nor is there furniture in the
patron's section of the bar. The proprietor uses a separate entrance and does business from behind bul-
letproof glass through a lazy Susan, while the male
patrons lean against the opposite wall drinking bottles of fortified wine and malt liquor.

As he was collecting his change, Haynes felt
someone brush his right shoulder. He found out later
that he had been marked on the back of his shoulder
with white chalk. This was once a common mugger's gambit, by which an accomplice of the muggers—who waited outside—marked the back of a
patron carrying a lot of dough.

As Haynes emerged from the bar he was grabbed
around the neck from behind by a larger, younger man
and approached by a smaller man who demanded his
money. Haynes threw his weight against the strong-
arm man as he did a front snap-kick to the chin of the
talker, knocking him to the ground in a daze.

The strong-arm man then said, "Oh, so you is a
fighta," and began cranking the hold as he and
Haynes fell back against the wall. As they struggled
against the wall, Haynes reached into his right front
pants pocket and drew his trusty barlow, with "nary
a click," reversed grip, stepped to the left, and drove
the blade "bone deep" into the mugger's thigh.

"The fool scream like a stuck pig, let go, fall to
da ground, and say, 'Please missa'—it was missa
now!—and beg, 'please don' kill me.'"

Haynes "turned about, flipped the barlow back,"
and said, "Naw, I ain't gonna kill ya, boy. But damn
if you eva gonna waylay anotha brutha."

(Haynes later confided to the author: "Ain't nothin' racial 'bout it. But, damm, there's plenny oh money to be had without robbin' a brutha! Weren't like that back home.")

As Haynes prepared to dish out "justice" with his trusty blade, the small man regained his feet and fled.

The larger man was curled in a half-fetal position trying to stem the flow of blood from his leg as Haynes spread his legs, got low (he demonstrated this to the author), and "filaayed his black ass!" For what Haynes reckoned as minutes (probably 10 to 15 seconds), he applied various shallow pressure cuts as his would-be mugger "squirm like a bitch and pled for mercy."

As Haynes began to roll his victim over to expose some fresh meat, his buddies swarmed about him, "drug me from the boy," and said, "Come on, man. That's enough. Don' kill 'im!"

Haynes complied, straightened up, and said, "It's cool. I'm all right."

When the boys let him go, he flipped the blade back over to the ice-pick hold and charged in, stabbing the grounded mugger.

Haynes' buddies once again restrained him, and disarmed him as well. He straightened up, took a deep breath, and said, "It's cool. I'm all right."

When the boys let him go, the whining of the mugger irritated him so that "I reached into my jacket pocket, take out my hook knife (a wicked carpet-laying tool), en cut his cryin' ass!" (Haynes demonstrated this cut as a leading inward stroke.)

Haynes was once again restrained by his friends just as the cops rolled up. His friends promptly disarmed him and did not let him go when he again said, "It's cool. I'm all right."

The cops had been looking for the mugger and his accomplice, because they were wanted for similar crimes and were in violation of parole. The cop told Haynes, "I don't know you. I want him."

Haynes, who was not then in possession of a blade, was told to cool off. At some point in the future one of the cops informed him of the surgical fate of the strong-arm man and that he had been "put away" on an unrelated charge.

As for the talker? Haynes ran into him at a later date. But that's a story that is best discussed in the context of blunt-force applications. You haven't heard the last of Haynes.

Well, there is an excellent—albeit bizarre—example of integrated fighting (empty hand and armed) as well as integrated weapon use: stab, cut, and slice from the overhand, ready, and lead. Haynes has since been arrested for beating up three young punks who tried to rob him at a bus stop.

LOCK BLADE

The folding lock blade is absolutely the most common blade out there. There is not a single working day that does not bring me within reach of a man—usually some kind of skilled laborer—who wears a folder on his belt in a snap case. Consequently, these things end up being pulled during the course of an altercation as often as razors, in contrast to your bigger blades, which are primarily employed in premeditated acts.

At 18 years of age I had just moved to Baltimore and was rooming with Ron Bone, a huge independent biker. He really wasn't a biker at all—hell, he road a Yamaha XT-500—but he was so big and so cool that the local bikers always invited him to hang out. On our way into this one particular establishment one night, we were halted by the bouncer and asked to turn over our blades, as he motioned to a shelf above the coat rack heaped with folders. Of course, we didn't carry blades at the time. We felt like real weenies when we had to confess our unarmed status to the bouncer. Ron Bone turned to me and said, "Remind me not to get in a fight on the parking lot."

In Baltimore, the guys renowned for carrying and using the folding lock blade are the Lumbee Indians of Butchers Hill on the East Side. They are typically about 5 feet, 8 inches, and 160 pounds, are copper-skinned with short hair, and often work as drywall hangers. They are natives of "Lumberton," a reservation outside Fayetteville, North Carolina. Young men who run afoul of the law down south tend to "immigrate" to Baltimore. Likewise, those who get in trouble in Baltimore head south.

To illustrate the point of the folder's being used during an escalating altercation, I reintroduce Russell, the menacing career felon from whom I saved Nate in Chapter 1. Both of these incidents occurred on the East Side.

Russell is built like a young George Foreman and appears at first glance to either be a Samoan or the largest Puerto Rican on the planet. He has enormous thighs and walks as fast as most men run. He is, in fact, a "breed," being part Cherokee. He has spent half his adult life behind bars, where he obviously takes advantage of the weight-training facilities.

A few months ago, Russel was spotted crossing Eastern Avenue on his way to the nearest emergency room. He had just finished drinking with Kane, a Lumbee who is said to be a loner and is not known to look for trouble. Russell was sporting a 6- to 12-inch cut across his chest (very similar to the slice inflicted by Mike on the Rambo-knife-wielding punk in Chris Pfouts' book, *True Tales of American Violence*), which he claimed was inflicted by Kane during an argument.

Now, knowing Russell—and knowing that he is twice the size of the average Lumbee—leads me to suspect that said argument involved Russell grabbing Kane. Russell has better than an 80-inch reach, which means that Kane was within grappling range when he inflicted what was obviously a slice. A single slice, which does not change directions, and is not accompanied by stabs or cuts, usually constitutes a warning. Against Russell, who is known to fight the cops, this is probably the mildest effective warning possible. The fact that Russell expressed no ill will toward Kane is all the verification I need for this story. When it comes to blade encounters, people with records tend to hold back information.

The following incident demonstrates the most common form of escalation involving the ubiquitous lock blade.

ON THE BAR LOT

Incident #50-01
Time of occurrence: night
Duration: 10–30 seconds
Perspective: eyewitness

Two drunks were fistfighting between their parked cars when the one who "was getting the worst of it" drew "a Buck folder, the typical 3 1/2-incher" and stabbed the larger man five times in the chest. Nearly a decade later, the stabbing victim is still undergoing therapy to rehabilitate a lung. There was no arrest or legal action involved with this incident.

In many such cases the blade seems to go up the centerline.

A folder deployed from a front pocket during a brawl will be used to stab up the center under the ribs.

Blades taken from the back pocket tend to be used for an inward turning stab or a cut to the left side of the body. Those pulled from cases are just as likely to go either way. The front pocket offers the most concealment for small blades.

THROWING THE BLADE

Every knife-fighting guru says not to throw knives. And in general I agree with this bit of wisdom. However, I never expected to encounter someone who had experience from either end of a knife throw—let alone both!

OWEN AND LES

Incident #52-24
Time of occurrence: night
Duration: 5 seconds
Perspective: first-person defender

Owen, "who was known to stab people," was having a drink at Les' place when he "went off," pulled his folder, and took a swipe at Les from the lead. As Owen leaned in for a stab, Les grabbed the blade with his right hand, only to have Owen draw back the blade, slicing open Les' hand. Les turned and ran for another room. As he looked over his shoulder he saw Owen toss the knife, which struck him butt-end first in the small of the back . . . (continued in Chapter 8).

THE BEACH BURGLAR

Incident #52-26
Time of occurrence: day
Duration: 3–4 seconds
Perspective: first-person aggressor

Les and his girl were enjoying the surf in Ocean City, Maryland, when he noticed a thief making off with their cooler. By the time Les had gotten back to knee-deep water, the thief had returned and was gathering up their clothes and blankets. Les drew his folder from the pocket of his cut-off jeans and made a good toss at the thief, striking him between the shoulder blades with an audible thud. The thief dropped the goods, picked up the blade, tossed it out to sea, and made his escape as Les came ashore.

For once my research does not contradict the generally accepted self-defense doctrine.

THE PENKNIFE

The penknife, not generally regarded as a weapon, is available in staggering varieties, most appearing to be quite harmless. It seems that nobody—from the slimy politicians who impinge on our every freedom and their mindless slaves in law enforcement to the deluded martial arts master fleecing his image-worshipping students to the serious blade artists who pen the rare useful book—considers the pen-knife a threat. And until I took a hard look at this subject, neither did I.

I think you will be surprised when you examine the stats at the end of this chapter. In general, the penknife conforms to the weapon use trends I delineated in Chapter 1: it's not much of a weapon and does not inspire confidence in the mind of the user, so it tends to be used in ruthless stealth attacks in strict accordance with its mechanical limitations, primarily like a razor.

My former landlord, a woman in her 30s, went off the deep end and killed her three young sons with a penknife and then used the blade to take her own life. I included only the killing of her oldest boy in this study because he was the only one who resisted—or was even capable of resisting—her ruthless attack.

Like the box cutter, the seemingly innocuous penknife becomes a deadly weapon in the hands of a maniac. But like any weapon, it also has lethal potential in the hands of an angel of mercy.

SWEET SANDY

Incident #51-15
Time of occurrence: day
Duration: seconds
Perspective: first-person defender

Dan was the son of a savage journeyman prizefighter. Growing up in the Pittsburgh area was a daily adventure for this young athlete who had been boxing and wrestling since age 5. At age 7, Dan was recruited by a 12-year-old by the name of Scott to fight other children for bets. These miniature bareknuckle bouts were seldom bloody because of the weak opposition and made plenty of money—in the form of bets—for Dan's handler.

By the time Dan turned 13 he had engaged in more than 100 such bouts, 25 of which were against a larger, older, mentally disturbed boy called Sted. These were Dan's only competitive bouts, though he won nearly all.

On one occasion, Sted was bullying some of Dan's friends at the park. Dan intervened, told Sted to leave, and turned to walk away, only to have Sted jump on his back in an insane fit of rage. Things went from bad to worse in a hurry as Sted locked a vicious choke hold on Dan and began to crank it like a maniac. Dan truly thought he was going to die as he saw stars and began to fade from lack of oxygen. Just as Dan expected to black out he heard Sandy, "a short, fat, 14-year-old—as sweet as can be," com-

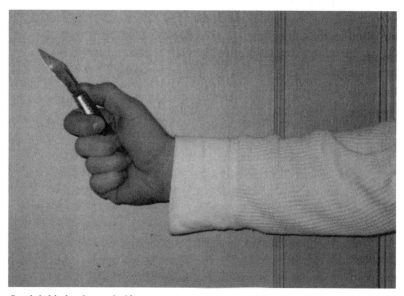

Sandy's blade, the penknife, was once a common tool for everyone.

mand Sted to "go home." Upon his release Dan saw
that Sandy had held her "little Barlow" to Sted's
throat. The touch of the blade had sent Sted on his
panicked flight home.

OVER A GIRL

Incident #52-16 & 17
Time of occurrence: night
Duration: minutes
Perspective: first-person defender

Les and his brother Jake were sitting on their
front porch not long after the next-door neighbor,
Josh, a young man about their age, had threatened
Les for dating a girl he fancied.

As Josh walked out his front door and turned
right to walk past them, Les felt "a hot, burning sensation" through his cheek and into his gums on the
left side of his face. As Josh passed Jake, who was
on Les' right, Les noticed a small keychain knife in
Josh's hand, which spurred Les to action.

Les jumped up and punched Josh in the face,
which caused Josh to lose his grip on the blade. As
it clattered across the sidewalk, Les tried to grab the
blade, only to have Josh kick it into the street. As
Josh ran back to his front door, followed by Jake and
Les, Josh's brother emerged with a bat.

While Jake fought Josh's brother barehanded,
both Les and Josh went into their houses to grab a
weapon. Josh emerged with a bat and Les with a
"long skinny pipe—real good for wackin'." The
brawl continued on the walk until the cops showed
up and arrested all four combatants, all of whom
were injured.

At this point it was discovered that Jake had had
his throat cut by Josh, although he hadn't felt a

thing. Josh and his brother had concussions. As for Les, the scar on his cheek is as long as my index finger and about an eighth of an inch wide.

"I looked in the mirror and could see my teeth through the side of my face, and where the gum was cut. I said, 'Goddam!' But they stitched it up right good."

Les got 30 days in jail. Jake was released. Josh and his brother got suspended sentences.

THE BALISONG

I have looked high and low for a switchblade, with no luck. It appears that the this bad-boy weapon of the 1960s and 1970s has been replaced by the balisong or butterfly knife. I have never thought much of the balisong as a weapon for three reasons:

- The initial deployment is relatively complex.
- It is the preferred blade of punks and wannabes.
- It is a "martial arts" weapon, which indicates that its use will favor visual impression over practical application. Theatrical imagery does not inspire fear or confidence in the mind of the serious fighter.

I must admit, though, that it seems to be one of those rare blades that is both effective and effective looking. And once you have studied the use of the blade to show and warn, you cannot discount visual impressions.

I own one of these knives—though not on purpose—and have forced myself to learn how to deploy it, despite my loathing it as an ego-projection device. I have abbreviated the deployment method taught me by my kali instructor. I am sure this has resulted in an artistic abomination. Apparently each style of Filipino blade fighting has its own preferred technique, all of which have been adopted by various Asian-American gangs as trademarks. Once again my methods appear brutish and oversimple compared to those of contemporary fighters.

Oh well, style is for fast women and the men who can afford them. . . .

TOMMY'S BOY

Incident #49-07
Time of occurrence: day
Duration: seconds
Perspective: first-person defender

Tommy, a young amateur boxer, and Alex, a respected friend, were approached by Andre, a younger, less respected associate. Andre had his butterfly knife predeployed and held low behind the hip as he approached at an angle, not doing a very god job of concealing the fact that he was concealing a weapon. There had been a previous disagreement regarding the holding of Tommy's gun. It appears that this incident had something to do with that discussion.

In any case Andre decided to rob his friends. When he made his demands, he brought the blade out next to his right hip, holding it at the ready, point up. Alex made a move for the weapon, which resulted in his receiving a cut that permanently disfigured his right hand. Tommy and Alex gave up their goods, and they still hang together. However, there is no mention of, or apparent animosity toward, Andre, against whom there was no legal action. All this leads me to believe that Andre has paid some kind of price for his crime.

BUTCHER KNIFE

A knife? Nah, not me, I've got a .357. I can't even stomach watching a man gut a deer.

—Ken

When someone comes for you with a butcher knife the operative word is *butcher*. Almost every case of butcher knife use I have documented has taken place in an urban environment. In fact, in the city you are just as likely to face a butcher knife as a folder. This is the weapon of choice for women and male dope fiends. It is the nonfolding knife to worry about. The butcher knife has been designed to permit your mother to dismember large animals. Think about it.

Like all tools used as cutting and stabbing weapons, the butcher knife is generally used in a practical manner by the untrained knifer. The person using the butcher knife is often extremely ruthless or unstable and is not concerned with the draw, since the weapon is already in his hand. The dynamics of the typical butcher knife attack emerge from the assailant's need to reduce the knife's visibility to third parties while approaching the target and to limit the length of the encounter. This typically results in a swift simultaneous approach/attack.

STOP, SHOP, & ROB

Incident #42-01
Time of occurrence: day
Duration: seconds
Perspective: news report

An off-duty cop doing security work at an inner city supermarket was stabbed in the back and shoulders by a female shoplifter wielding a butcher knife (an obvious use of the overhand). The cop managed to draw his weapon while being stabbed (if this had been a man doing a grab and stab the cop would have been toast) and shoot the woman in the leg, disabling her. The news report indicated that the cop was headed for some legal hassles.

(I got this one while watching *The Price Is Right* with my Grandma. Bob does have some nice babes.)

If at all possible, do yourself a favor and don't be the one who does society a favor.

—Marc "Animal" MacYoung

SHEATH KNIFE
("NO, *THIS* IS A KNIFE!")

The line delivered by Paul Hogan in *Crocodile Dundee* probably represents the most accurate motion picture depiction of knife use to date. (Nothing realistic ever happens in the martial arts flicks.) From the punk showing the blade to his confidence implosion when faced with a more menacing weapon, I'll bet my left one that this happens every day of the week somewhere in America. Knifers who expect to face an unarmed party (that would be 99 percent of them) always fare miserably when they come up against a determined armed party.

A poorly maintained scuba knife is useful for such tasks as cutting through rusty wire and scaring people, but it is not a practical combat blade. Just in case you have to fight two or more bags of meat, you do want to be able to extract your blade swiftly following a successful thrust. Having your blade hung up on a rib or jacket seam is not desirable in the heat of battle.

When it comes to sheath knives—especially the modern Rambo things with all the nasty teeth and sleek curves—you are talking about knives that were designed for show. And showing just happens to be what they are used for.

HONOR AND PATRIARCHY

Incident #19-21
Time of occurrence: night
Duration: seconds
Perspective: first-person aggressor

S.J. and Mike were really drunk as they pulled into the parking lot of what figured to be the last watering hole of the night. As they emerged from their car, they heard the sounds of a man beating a woman. Mike confronted the man, and S.J. came up behind him. When they tried to talk him out of beating the woman, he reached into his car and pulled out a bat.

S.J. was an accomplished martial artist, but he was so drunk he figured he was in for an ugly outing. As the thought of falling on his ass while attempting a kick crossed S.J.'s mind, Mike drew a large sheath knife. The wife beater immediately dropped the bat and pleaded for understanding. The maggot even followed the guys into the bar and offered to buy them a drink, the magnanimous loser of a brandishing contest.

"NO, THIS IS *NOT* A KNIFE"

Incident #52-28
Time of occurrence: day
Duration: minutes
Perspective: first-person defender

Jimmy was heading home from work one day when four jerks in the following car began threatening him. The driver had a "big fucking knife" that he was pointing at Jimmy, and twisting as if it were a screwdriver. This continued for quite some time. Finally, as Rambo Jr. pulled alongside, Jimmy placed his .45 auto on the dashboard in full view. The knife was not seen again.

THE MEAT CUTTER'S KNIFE

THE MEAT CUTTER'S WIFE

Incident #47-05, 06
Time of occurrence: night
Duration: 15–30 seconds
Perspective: eyewitness

Bernie, a former ballplayer and easygoing ladies' man, was having a drink at a "respectable joint" on Baltimore's West Side when the husband of a woman who was seated at the bar speaking with her boyfriend walked in.

The ensuing encounter was so terrifying that Bernie did his best to forget it and had a hard time reconstructing the action in any detail during my interview with him. It appears that the woman was seated with her back to the door and the bar to her left, speaking with a man seated to her front and facing in the opposite direction. (Whoever this guy was he certainly wasn't a hero—he took no part in the action—other than quickly vanishing from the scene.)

Without pausing, the husband walked up to his wife and made a deep curving upward slice below the right breast. There was a definite wrist motion with the knife hand that resulted in the separation of the breast, as the woman screamed and fled out the front door with her husband in pursuit.

Somehow the woman evaded the knifer and ran back into the bar, where a friend of Bernie attempted to help.

"All you seen was the knife glistenin'. It was scary. All you seen was a shiny knife en blood sizzlin'.

"He grabbed um, but didn't get the knife—the guy was good, real good; bad guy. I went to school with that guy—come from a bad area. He was a meat cutter—sliced half my friend's face off en took that woman's breast with one stroke.

"Someone said, 'Bernie, why don't you stop that?'

"I said, 'Nah, not me.'

"Bad dude. A lot of excitement. Know what I'm mad about? I left my drink on the bar. . . ."

Bernie does not know the fate of the woman or the knifer because he left to rush his wounded friend to the hospital. His friend's injury resulted in no police or legal activity.

MISCELLANEOUS KNIVES

This category includes steak knives, paring knives, hook knives, oddball cutlery, and anything I haven't thought of. It usually happens to be what's lying around when a crime of passion is in the making or when some exotic type of maniac hatches a low-end crime scheme, such as robbing a hotdog vendor. Before dismissing such diabolic acts based on the usual low mental competence of the perpetrator, one should first consider the nature of the deranged knifer.

The following scenario was related to me by Kenneth, a career security guard. I give it to you as faithfully transcribed on the scene by my own hand. This incident is similar to a fight with a female shoplifter that happened at my job the week before, except for two differences: my co-workers did not get police assistance, and Kenneth's babe did not (thank God) have a knife. Imagine if our female filcher below had had a blade and her opposition had consisted of two small women and two ordinary unarmed men. One must also keep in mind that the man who tells the following story has "beaten down" dozens of violent—and often armed—young men in his capacity as an armed security guard.

TWANNITA!

Incident #53-01
Time of occurrence: day
Duration: minutes
Perspective: first-person aggressor

"Oh, man! Today was terrible! The day job put a hurtin' on me today! Got ma ass whooped by a girl. No foolin'.

"She about 6 foot, 160, en young. I caught 'er leavin' with $60 worth a deodorants. Grab her from behind by the wrists and say, 'You unda arrest.' That bitch hit me—a punch, don't ya know [demonstrates left hook to jaw]. And then she pick me up [demonstrates suplex] and throw me to the floor—I two-ten! That's when the fear come. I said, 'Oh ma God, I got to fight this bitch for ma life!'

"We was rollin' on the floor, battlin', the both of us punchin' away. I was thinkin', 'What had I got myself into?' You know, when a woman pick you up en slam you, it take you by surprise. I generally be the one overpowerin' people. I figure if someone gonna pick me up en slam me it gonna be a man or one a those young hoppers, not a woman—a junkie yet!

"She was on somthin'. I had me a real woman on my hands. So much so that I forgot and fought like she were a man. I was goin' for it. But she was tearin' my ass up—whoopin my ass!

"People were laughin' 'bout me gettin' tore up by this woman—say'n I'm lucky she weren't ma wife, I'd be doin' laundry en so on. But when that cop showed en gone upside the back a her head with that stick she juss look at him like he was crazy. He were a short, muscular cop—the body-buildin' kind—en she pick his ass up by the neck with one hand en toss 'um [demonstrates Darth Vader elevator choke]. That's when the people watchin' got scared, figurin' she gone en kill somebody.

"A lady cop show up en go ta work with her stick, and they battlin'—losin' the battle. So I throw in with my stick. We workin' her—workin' this bitch good—and she stayin' strong, givin' it right back!

"We was goin' ta war on her [demonstrates two-handed stick strokes] upside her head. Blood everywhere, all about. She wasn't feelin' it. Didn't stop her.

"Four more cops come en she still fightin'. Took all six of um to cuff her—and she broke the cuffs. Even after they strap her to the stretcher she still fightin'.

"Oh Lord, I'm sore. Don't need another day like that. That woman, though, she goin' away for a long time. She need it."

A NOTE ON DOCUMENTATION: I recorded this event as four separate encounters: a one-on-one, a two-on-one, a three-on-one, and a seven-on-one. Abbreviating the coverage of such a shifting dynamic situation to a simple seven-to-one arrest would grossly distort the facts.

HOLDING BACK

Having interviewed the men who participated in these encounters, I am quite certain that their strong inhibitions against using force on a woman contributed to the temporary success of the bloodthirsty female felons. Cultural conditioning is a strong factor affecting the use of edged weapons. Keep an eye on this one. (Aggression inhibitors will be discussed at length later in this book.)

UNBALANCED WEAPON PERCEPTIONS

The previously mentioned encounter at my job that was similar to the above action became a four-on-one arrest of a 90-pound woman. The entire episode took minutes and involved the female's hurling a filled quart bottle and attacking with a paring knife, which remained in its retail package. I experimented with this packaged blade and determined that it would only pose a danger if someone had grabbed the packaging, permitting her to pull the blade free and use it. It would be impossible to drive the blade through the packaging into a body. Any such attempt would result in a bent package and broken blade or a loss of grip. Nevertheless, the cops based the armed robbery charge on the use of the packaged knife, not the quart bottle, which offered far more potential to harm under the circumstances.

The knife is the most taboo weapon in our culture. Americans are "distance killers." Of those potential lethal implements that are commonly recognized as weapons in our society (e.g., guns, bombs, knives), knives are used at the closest range and are hence the most personal choice. Of the three, knives also require the most risk and effort on the part of the user. To the modern mind, needless risk and

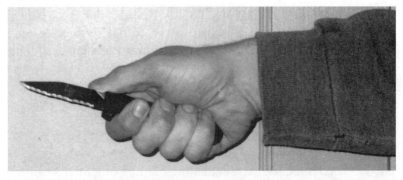

Unreliable weapons of desperation—such as this $1.79 paring knife, which projects a weak visual image—are most likely to be used in a practical, stealthy, and ruthless manner. This blade is gripped to deliver an inward stab and slice (or rip cut). It is classified along with steak, fish, carving, and linoleum knives as a miscellaneous fixed blade.

effort are often common grounds for doubting one's sanity. It is a hard fact that the popular culture will more readily accept the bombing of Third World children than the stabbing of a local law officer.

DOING IT IN STYLE

The knife is most definitely recognized and respected by all aggressors and defenders as a weapon to be reckoned with. This appears to inspire a wider—and often less effective—range of uses among the often mentally challenged knifer. It also seems to encourage the unarmed party to act in some reasonable fashion, in stark contrast to those who face razor users, shankers, and swordsmen. Those who face the very limited shank or razor often react as if they were the victim of a natural disaster: becoming paralyzed or disoriented. And, for unknown reasons, people tend to act aggressively against a man brandishing a sword, sometimes with disastrous results.

PLAYING STRAIGHT WITH THE NUMBERS

There is no objective truth. Life is a subjective mess. . . . Chaos is the rule. Order is a mathematical fantasy.
—Tattoo Rick

There are so many ways to slice any statistical survey that the pursuit is often meaningless. Although I am a novice, it has become obvious to me that I could present my findings in accord with various opinions and prejudices of mine so as to support those views. That is not my intention.

I am not a political pollster. I am trying to educate myself about the very serious business of getting bled, skinned, gutted, and boned. I can tell you that more than half of the opinions I have held—and estimates I have made—at the outset of my various studies have proven wrong. The effectiveness of blunt weapons, throws by untrained fighters, and attacks by individuals on groups were a surprise to me, even though I was the one who collected every scrap of information. The fact that I held certain views warped my processing of the information I was gathering.

I am aware of my own ignorance. This study is not an attempt to push my misconceptions, but to right them. It's a personal endeavor. I do not expect my fellow martial artists to abandon their delusions for the truth. My quest for the facts associated with filleting our fellow man is purely selfish.

Simply the way we count blade usage is a huge variable. I have my choice of six denominators:

1. Acts of violence involving a blade or shank
2. Parties armed with a blade or shank
3. Blade or shank deployments
4. Attempts to injure with a blade or shank
5. Various uses of the blade or shank, some of which are not injury attempts
6. The use postures utilized by an armed individual

Sticking with number one glosses over a lot. Going with number six leaves me guessing in too many cases.

My primary denominators will be deployments and uses. Acts and parties are only adequate for comparisons of different types of weapons (likes clubs versus guns) and to note general trends. Injury attempts and use postures are extremely important to pin down but are more easily understood as (and more accurately the results of) deployments and uses than as causes.

Blade use tends to be pretty one-dimensional—one way all the way, stab, stab, stab, stab! In the case of razors, shanks, and swords the extreme nature and limitations of the weapons amplify this factor. Most of the numbers and variations in blade use are to be found in the knife category. Hence, this attempt to get the numbers right in this chapter.

NOTE: If some yo-yo flips his blade over to the ice pick and back to the lead 10 times, that's only two variations in posture, not 20.

OF 190 KNIFE USES (PERCENTAGES)

Blade	% Deployments	Hold	TECHNIQUES						POSTURES		
			Show	Warn	Throw	Slash	Slice	Stab	Over	Lead	Ready
Folder	61	7	22	9	2	23	9	36	4	32	64
Pen	4	-	25	13	-	25	13	25	-	38	62
Lock	47	7	17	10	2	22	10	39	4	30	64
Bali	5	22	33	11	-	-	11	22	12	44	44
Switch	5	-	45	-	-	45	-	27	-	36	64
Fixed	39	4	18	1	-	16	11	57	27	36	37
Butcher[1]	20	5	13	3	-	11	8	61	29	29	42
Sheath[2]	11	5	33	-	-	14	24	43	29	33	38
Misc.[3]	8	-	7	-	-	33	7	67	25	50	25

NOTES

1. Butcher knives include home and commercial meat-cutting tools.
2. Sheath knives include sheathed blades of the military and sporting variety, excluding Bowies, Arkansas toothpicks, and anything else heavy enough to use as a club while sheathed.
3. Miscellaneous knives include hook knives, paring knives, steak knives, fish knives, and any other kitchen or workplace cutlery not heavy enough to chop through bone or frozen meats.

OF 139 KNIFE-ARMED AGGRESSIONS (PERCENTAGES)

Blade	% Deployments	ARMED AGGRESSOR					DEFENDER					
		Grp.	KO'd	Med.	Leg.	Dth.	Armed	Grp.	KO'd	Med.	Leg.	Dth.
Folder	60	24	4	5%	24	2	12	11	19	61	1	12
Pen	4	-	-	20	20	-	20	-	20	60	20	20
Lock	48	28	4	4	24	1	8	12	16	63	1	10
Balisong	3	25	-	-	-	-	-	25	-	25	-	-
Switch	6	-	13	13	38	13	38	-	50	63	-	25
Fixed	40	16	7	11	47	-	18	5	38	69	2	22
Butcher	20	11	4	7	57	-	7	-	50	68	-	39
Sheath	12	6	12	6	35	-	35	12	24	59	-	6
Misc.	7	-	10	30	40	-	20	10	30	90	10	-

OF 51 KNIFE-ARMED DEFENSES
(SHOWN IN PERCENTS)

Blade	% Deployments	ARMED DEFENDER					AGGRESSOR					
		Grp.	KO'd	Med.	Leg.	Dth.	Armed	Grp.	KO'd	Med.	Leg.	Dth.
Folder	67	12	15	21	21	3	29	26	26	44	3	9
Pen	4	-	-	50	-	-	50	-	-	50	-	-
Lock	47	13	17	25	33	4	21	33	33	50	4	8
Balisong	10	20	20	-	-	20	20	20	40	-	20	
Switch	6	-	33	33	-	-	100	-	-	-	-	-
Fixed	33	6	12	24	29	6	47	41	29	59	18	
Butcher	15	13	26	26	26	13	50	63	38	50	-	-
Sheath	10	-	-	-	-	-	40	20	40	60	20	-
Misc.	8	25	-	50	75	-	50	25	-	75	50	-

CHAPTER 7

Bloody Junk
The Nature and Use of Shanks

It was crazy. He stabbed him so many times you couldn't count—like this [short, fast downward ice-pick stabs from the elbow]. The yellow coveralls soaked [the blood] up like this [spreads fingers of right hand slowly over left shoulder]. He kept on stabbing until his knees buckled and then stabbed him some more . . . looked me square in the eye. I just looked down [imitates with a shoulder shrug] and stepped around. Didn't want any of that.

—Raphael

In some parts of the country *shank* is a generic term for the blade. In Baltimore we don't call knives shanks often, but we refer to being cut or stabbed as being "shanked." The popular culture associates shank use with our wonderful penal system. This is a very accurate association. Although I have interviewed some former inmates, corrections officers, and construction workers about shank use in prison, much of my information on the use of improvised stabbing weapons comes from grisly events experienced on "the outside." I define shanks as improvised stabbing weapons without a cutting edge.

LETTING GO

That's true," I said, "if you're only practicing, jabbing your point into a tree or something of that kind. But in a real fight, a thrown weapon always strikes harder. Something makes us hold back, if only a little, when we strike another man. To strike hard at the back of one who has already been knocked down is particularly difficult.

—Gene Wolfe, *Soldier of Arete*

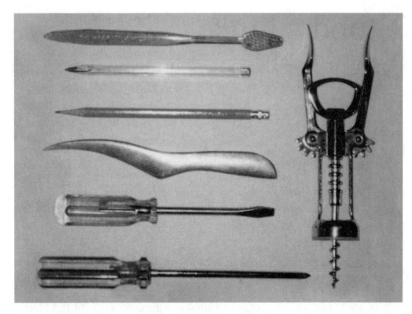

Assorted shanks. The most common shank (outside of corrections facilities) is the pencil; the best penetrator is the Phillips head screwdriver.

The above writer is a master of speculative fiction. If he is, or ever has been, a fighter, I do not know. Although he often writes from the perspective of some death dealer—a torturer, a sacrificing priest, or, in the above case, a professional fighting man—his work never dwells on the gory act or combat dynamics. "Hewed" limbs and heads, "gore-spattered" blades, "spilled entrails," and heroes wading through pools of enemy blood are not features of his work. His stuff has a religious feel. And the central character has to cope with the realization of his brutal past, present, or future.

If you've been in real fights, have associated closely with over-experienced fighting men (e.g., prizefighters, combat veterans), or have honestly tried to do in your fellow man, I doubt if you have dozed off during the preceding paragraph. I realized early on in my pursuit of fighting ability that most martial artists do not understand the true martial figure, the fighter—what buoys his fears and doubts and keeps him from descending into insanity. The true study of fighters is the study of the fighter's character, not his technique.

The focus on mechanical and theatrical minutiae is the hallmark of the modern martial artist. Trying to find the secret to success in combat through studying "the moves of the masters" is like trying to achieve an understanding of a *Playboy* Playmate's beauty by analyzing the gauge, grade, and gloss of the paper on which her picture is printed.

The fictional—though insightful—quote that began this segment centered on the discussion of the wounds suffered by King Leonidas of Sparta at the legendary Battle of Thermopylae (the "hot gates" in Greek), a coastal pass at which he and 300 selected Spartans with living male heirs (a suicide battalion) and a few thousand Greek allies attempted to stop the army of Xerxes, the great king of Persia, whose host numbered between 30,000 and 300,000, depending on who's telling the story.

On the final day Leonidas, his surviving Spartan Peers (the toughest bisexuals in history), and their remaining squires were among the final 400 defenders betrayed by locals and surrounded by the Persian force, which included a select body of 10,000 Immortals (fanatical royal bodyguards). Needless to say, the heroes died in gory style, taking a lot of pretty tough hombres with them (anyone who marches halfway across the known world to fight heavily armed gay-rights activists with sharp sticks is tough) and ruining a lot of fancy costumes in the process.

The point is, if Leonidas were to hop on a time machine and appear at Parris Island (U.S. Marine Corps boot camp in South Carolina) or Fort Bragg (U.S. Army Special Forces camp in North Carolina), he would know that he was in the presence of fighting men: mere peltasts (skirmishers), but fighting men all the same. If he appeared in a boxing gym, he would certainly recognize the athletes as fighting men, if not soldiers. Should he appear on the line of scrimmage at an National Football League game he would think himself on an Olympian field of battle. If the ancient king showed up in the yard of a U.S. prison he would see fighting men—albeit barbarians—all around. However, should the hero of "the hot gates" appear at a modern martial arts school or tournament, he would surely think that he had been banished to the Athenian theater or exiled to the isle of Lesbos.

I treasure the martial arts and seek to find good in their modern forms at every turn. Indeed, I have written a book on how one can use the martial arts to increase the chances of surviving serious self-defense situations as well as brainless brawls. However, in the context of blade and shank fighting, I cannot place enough emphasis on the phony nature of such arts as practiced today, especially in regard to the shank. You see, when it comes to the knife, the razor, or the sword, the weapon is the focus. Not so with the shank. The shanker, in 99 percent of instances, has let go and is about to achieve that maximum penetration that Latro (the protagonist of Wolfe's novel) points out is so unnatural to a man struggling with another man.

The answer is clear. The shanker is emotionally unhinged or has succeeded in dehumanizing his antagonist or victim to the point that he might as well be jabbing a piece of wood. In the previous chapter, I made the point that while knife victims tend to react reasonably, shank victims behave more like panic-stricken victims of a natural disaster than like a combatant, rational or not. Again, the focus of terror is not the screwdriver, ice pick, or pencil being used, but the behavior of the user. To understand and deal with that level of aggression, one must have faced it previously, ideally under controlled circumstances, such as in combat sports, law enforcement, or security work.

Since the mid-1980s I've been training approximately one novice boxer per year. Some have been young athletes, some ordinary folks, and some martial artists. The athletes and everyday people approached me as a coach and became my training partners. The martial artists approached me as a training partner and soon became my students. A properly oriented aspiring athlete—with no training, experience, or unusual natural abilities—is more capable of defending himself the first day he walks into a gym than a graduating karate black belt is when he accepts his certificate of achievement.

The dynamics here are actually quite simple, although it's exacerbated by the tendency of martial arts systems to dull our natural instincts and instill poor combat orientation. Grasping this simple concept is key to fighting for your life.

There are two primary aggression inhibitors:

- Fear of harm to oneself
- Fear of harm to one's antagonist

The second fear is deeply ingrained in a nonfighter and never comes into play until one overcomes fear of harm. I have noticed that women and male martial artists with whom I have trained show a high degree of flinching, hesitation, and other signs of inhibited aggression. If you have never feared harming your adversary in a gym bout, athletic contest, or brawl, you are either insane or stone-cold cruel, or you have never overcome your primary selfish fear of injury.

If you have spent any time among prizefighters in the gym or football players on the gridiron, you will have recognized two types of effective combatants:

1. *The finesse athletes who have no fear for their own hide but sometimes hold back out of fear for others.* These are the stylistic defensive boxers who seem to lack the killer instinct and the offensive backfield personified by the fearless and self-sacrificing—but hardly feared—quarterback and his wide receiver.
2. *The pressure athletes or "killers" who know no fear but the fear of failing to dominate their opposition.* In the ring you're talking about the Mike Tysons who seem driven to destroy, and on the football field anybody on defense or the line of scrimmage fits this category, with the defensive linebacker personifying the apex predator on the ballfield.

In the epic drugstore fracas between Kenneth and Twannita related in the previous chapter, you had a perfect misalignment of these two phenomena. Kenneth had as little fear of personal injury as is reasonable but really held back—despite his protests that he fought all out—out of his reverence for women as noncombatants. To overcome such a complex and ingrained emotion is no easy trick and has been the focus of warrior societies (such as the Norse Berserkers) since the dawn of armed conflict.

On the other hand Twannita, who, as a modern American female and member of the black underclass has been taught since infancy

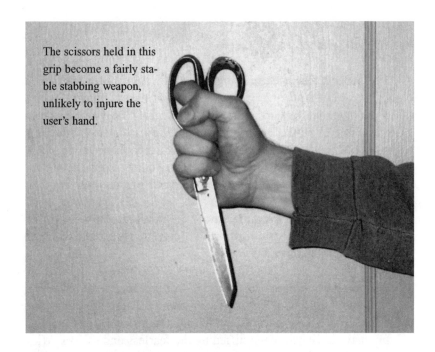

The scissors held in this grip become a fairly stable stabbing weapon, unlikely to injure the user's hand.

that men are subhuman predators and who has not had the physical capacity through most of her young life to harm men, has no ingrained fear that she will harm a man. She need only overcome her basic fear of injury, which is easy enough if you're flying on an $80 ticket with Crack Airlines.

Striking an internal balance between these two natural fears is the proper focus of self-defense study. All the techniques and weapon skills in the vast martial arts arsenal will not save your tail (or that of your partner's) if you're frozen in slack-jawed terror. Remember, the shanker has already mentally slotted you somewhere between the lunchmeat drawer in his refrigerator and his cat's litter box. And whatever crude tool he has chosen to fulfill his vision of your future is not a mental crutch, an ego projection device, or even something he'd bother bringing in out of the rain.

Then again there are the eternal sociopaths among us who see a weapon at every turn. . . .

GETTING SCREWED

Incident #39-12
Time of occurrence: day
Duration: 4 seconds
Perspective: eyewitness

Raphael and four other members of the Almighty Nation of the Latin Kings were drinking beer in a private garage. . . .

"The next thing I know Leon, known as 'Animal' in the 'hood and among the Kings, and Jesse, a punk, were arguing and cussing. Leon walks over to the tool box, grabs a screwdriver—a flathead, I think—walks up to Jesse, and punches him below the ribs on his left side. (I thought it was a punch. It sounded like a punch.) He put his left hand on Jesse's chest and kind of pushed him to the floor while he hit him three more times. Jesse just groaned and held his side. And Leon said, 'What do you think about that? I fixed your ass, didn't I?'

"I thought it was hilarious. I don't know why. We just started laughing. We finished our beer and left, and called an ambulance after we left. Jesse had to have a colostomy. I visited him, and no way was he putting the finger on Leon. The police made an inquiry into the incident, but nobody was talking. We were Kings.

"Leon was always like that. He's a sick puppy. When I was in the army he got married. When I came back he was a different person. His wife put a gun to his head and straightened him out."

DUZ

Incident #03-22
Time of occurrence: day
Duration: seconds
Perspective: eyewitness

"Duz was real laid-back in school—that intense kind of quiet that jerks can't stand. One day this idiot says something about his mother in class, and Duz dives across the classroom, tackles the guy, and stabs him through the ear with a pencil.

"Way to go, Duz. It was brutal."

LIFE AS A WINE CORK

Incident #41-06
Time of occurrence: day
Duration: minute plus
Perspective: first-person defender

"This was in ninth grade. I was 6-2, maybe 140—a tall, skinny kid. A friend of mine told me that this guy had threatened his friend John, and asked if I would walk him home in case he got jumped.

"The guy after him was a small bully who could basically do anything he wanted because everybody was afraid of his older brothers, who were also bullies. Everybody but me. I've fought all my life. With him, if it came to a fight, it was with the knife or a corkscrew. I didn't know that before the fight.

"We were walking down Fort Avenue from Locust Point. I was on the sidewalk side of the sidewalk, and John was on the street side. Milton was standing on these steps. He jumped off the steps in front of me, and John got behind me. He hit me in the lip. [The corkscrew] went through the lip, off the

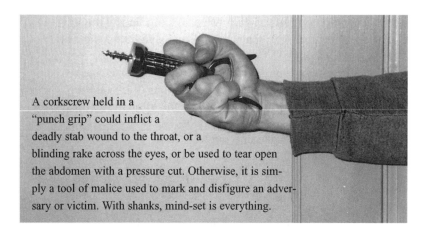

A corkscrew held in a "punch grip" could inflict a deadly stab wound to the throat, or a blinding rake across the eyes, or be used to tear open the abdomen with a pressure cut. Otherwise, it is simply a tool of malice used to mark and disfigure an adversary or victim. With shanks, mind-set is everything.

teeth, and into the gum on the right side of the mouth. I didn't feel a thing—never do. It's kind of shocking mentally that they have enough balls to hit me. Like they were that fucking stupid. That kind of stupidity is always surprising.

"My first instinct is to grab my victim. They're always the victim. I like to grab people so that they can't run away—don't want them to get away. It might start out with two or three of um, like an attack, but it's only a matter of time. He was hitting me in the side under the arm, and I thought that was kind of strange. You know there's nothin' there. You don't hurt somebody there.

"I put my left arm under his right arm, brought it over his shoulder back in front under his chin, bent his head back, and pile-drived him in the face with my right fist about three times before I noticed he was stabb'n me. I didn't know he was stabb'n me until I saw the fibers of my shirt floating up in front of my face—my favorite shirt. Was my favorite shirt.

"I grabbed his left wrist with my right hand, his elbow with my left, and twisted it back to the outside over his shoulder. He had to let go or the shoulder was going to pop—ooh, yeah—he let go of the corkscrew right away. Then I spun him around, grabbed his head from behind, and slammed his face into a new LTD. You always want to slam the face. It hurts more than the back of the head. I started at the trunk above the rear bumper, bounced his face up over the trunk, the rear glass, the roof, down the windshield, and across the hood.

"The owner came out and started cryin' that I was ruining his paint job. So I pulled his head up until his feet came off the ground, stepped back, and threw him down to my right. It was a controlled flip. You want to let go at the last possible moment so the part that you want to hit hits. You want the head to hit the pavement. That's the whole object of the game. If done properly, it sounds like a coconut. Pick up a coconut sometime and throw it down. Kind of an empty, hollow sound.

"Including the stab through the lip he got me nine times. There was no meat hangin' out, so I taped 'um up, and they healed fine. Oh, him? I just told him how it was and went on my way. The other guy [John] he was definitely pleased with the outcome. Don't know if he [Milton] was hurt. He was sleep'n when I left. The car owner, though, he wasn't happy. There was blood on the LTD. His brothers didn't fuck with me. They knew better. He's been my friend since the fight. Know him real well."

EDDIE THE BUTCHER

Incident #52-19 & 20
Time of occurrence: night
Duration: minutes
Perspective: secondhand account related by the butcher's cellmate

Eddie and his "homeboy" were miffed at a fellow consumer of illicit drugs. Having seen too many gangster movies, no doubt, they "took their boy for a ride" to a wooded area, where Eddie stabbed him repeatedly with a screwdriver and interred him in a shallow grave. The next day Eddie's "homeboy" confided in his mentor that he didn't think the guy was dead. That night our dynamic duo hopped back into their "ride," returned to the burial site, and "dug the guy up and stabbed him in the head with the screwdriver." They were arrested and convicted for murder based on the testimony of an eyewitness who only saw their ghoulish return to the scene of the original crime.

ON THE INSIDE

I worked down at Baltimore City Jail for two years. The place is falling apart, roaches behind every panel. The material is so deteriorated from everybody pissing on it that the 1x1 angle irons are easily pried out.

They hide the shit under the rim of the toilets where we had to caulk. I found a shank made of looped wire and white medical tape. one was a 1/4-inch steel bar that was 10 inches long and had been sharpened to a point—that was a lot of work, whoever did that. I also found an 1/8-inch nail punch. You just turn the stuff in, that's it. You don't want to get involved with finger pointing.

Their in-house maintenance is terrible. The beds are steel frame, and you can see where they break pieces off. Old pipe is left lying around. It's a hellhole. I must've lost three or four tools down there. At least two screwdrivers. What am I going to do? Have them lock the whole place down while I look for a screwdriver? I go buy another one. Hell, they're so lax anyhow. They barely pat these guys down when they come back off the highway details. They could pick up anything out there. The worst ones are the juveniles. The older ones are laid back—talk about their girls, pass us pictures through the grate. The punks, though, they're out of hand. I told a couple how it was going to be if they started with me. We torched one through the grill of his cell.

—Kirk, a low-profile construction worker

THE BUTCHER THROWS A PARTY

Incident #52-27
Time of occurrence: day
Duration: minute plus
Perspective: eyewitness

"These four macho weight-lifter guys came in from the yard and attacked this guy on the tier. While the three big ones were beating this guy with their hands, Eddie was stabbing him with a pair of scissors 'til the scissors broke off in the guy's neck. They went on their way, and the guy died right there. None of those guys were fingered."

IN THE YARD

Incident #52-21
Time of occurrence: day
Duration: 30–40 seconds
Perspective: eyewitness

"Out in the courtyard I heard the sound of a baseball being hit. I said, 'Damn, he must've hit that ball good. I got to see this!' When I looked across the yard to where the sound came from, I saw this guy swinging his bat at this other guy whose head was split open. The guy with the split head staggered back and flipped out a shank, holds it like this [in the ready below right ribs], and stabs this guy in the chest.

"They fought for a while before the guards came. No grabbing or wrestling, just moving and striking. The guy with the bat got in a couple more hits and was stabbed maybe four more times. Both guys collapsed and were taken out. The knife guy was definitely worse off. His whole head was split open.

"Most of the action on the tiers is not punished.

The knife guy just passes the weapon along. But the yard is different."

ON THE TIER

Incident #52-22
Time of occurrence: day
Duration: 20–30 seconds
Perspective: eyewitness

A large inmate attacked a smaller inmate with a shank held in the overhand. As the defender attempted to run and dodge, the attacker stabbed him between 15 and 20 times to the hand, head, and shoulders. Guards rescued the victim, who recovered from his wounds. The attacker got some more time.

IN THE CELL

Incident #52-23
Time of occurrence: night
Duration: minutes
Perspective: secondhand account from a resident of the tier who heard the action and aftermath

An inmate stabbed his cell-mate to death while he lay in his bunk (obvious use of the overhand) and hung him up. When the guards came to check the cell the next morning he was cutting a piece out of the cadaver and eating it raw.

WEAPONS OF MASS DESTRUCTION FOR THE PETTY THIEF

I firmly believe that, if there was a nuclear warhead that could be fixed to the tip of a stick, such a device would be used to stab people during an arrest, drunken brawl, or domestic altercation.

BIOHAZARD IN AISLE 10

Incident #49-20
Time of occurrence: day
Duration: 10–20 seconds
Perspective: eyewitness

A shoplifter was surrounded by five plain-clothes security guards ("store detectives") and informed that he was under arrest. He then produced a syringe, yelled, 'I have AIDS!' and attacked the nearest guard with a lunging lead-hand thrust. He was promptly brought down by the five officers who had a hard time cuffing him. During the resulting floor fight one of the guards received a nasty bite.

In terms of biological combat, I suppose the junkie was feinting with one delivery system (the syringe) and injecting his lethal agent through an alternative system (his teeth).

OF 30 ACTS OF SHANK USE
(PERCENTAGES)

Weapon	% Use	TECHNIQUES				POSTURES		
		Hold	Show	Warn	Stab	Lead	Ready	Overhand
Common[1]	27	-	-	-	100	-	37	63
Tools[2]	30	-	11	-	89	-	78	22
Shanks[3]	37	-	-	-	100	-	64	36
Syringe	6	-	50	-	50	50	50	-

NOTES

1. Common items such as pencils, pens, broken beer bottles.
2. Screwdrivers, scissors, corkscrews, ice picks, etc.
3. Prison-made shanks.

Weapon	SHANK-ARMED AGGRESSOR					ANTAGONIST				
	Group	KO'd	Med.	Leg.	Dth.	Armed	KO'd	Med.	Leg.	Dth.
Common	-	13	13	13	-	-	13	100	-	13
Tolls	44	11	11	27	-	11	44	78	33	22
Shanks	27	-	-	55	-	-	64	73	-	55

NOTE

The bat-against-shank prison yard fight related in this chapter is the only known case of a shank-armed defender. Even in this case one cannot discount the possibility that the bat man was launching a preemptive strike against a shank-armed assassin stalking him in the yard.

CHAPTER 8

Awesome but Obsolete
The Nature and Use of Modern Swords

*Your bolts and bars are
strong, but I always sleep with
steel by my side.*
—Robert E. Howard,
Conan: Shadows in Zamboula

I may have better manners than the fictional barbarian swords-man, but I too sleep with steel by my side: the Bowie's on the right side of the bed, the machete's on the left, and the sword is sheathed next to the door. Since beginning the Violence Project, I have been relieved to discover that I'm not the only guy with one of these things between the mattress and the box springs. The sword continues to fascinate the modern mind, and it is, on a practical level, a superb home-defense weapon.

Sword arts, both Asian and Western, are currently enjoying a surge of interest among U.S. marital artists. And about once a year, you see or hear in the news about some nut robbing a hamburger joint with a ninja sword. I'm as fascinated by the sword as the next man. Emotionally, it's an easy weapon. If you know how to use it— and therefore know how ridiculous the martial arts sword-disarming techniques are—your confidence will swell when it's in your hand. Also, you don't have to worry about accidentally discharging the thing in the dark and blowing away your drunken brother-in-law who lost his key.

As a teen I participated in medieval-style battles and duels with padded wooden swords, spears, and dirks. If you read my first book, *The Fighting Edge*, you know the rest. I made a real 7-pound steel sword, practiced with it, and eventually used it. This all resulted in some legal hassles of the first magnitude. After my father, his lawyer, and the cop saved my ass, I was told to leave the state to avoid civil retaliation. I did.

I have recently become interested in how people recall past violence. So I am going to use this topic to do a little comparative storytelling. Three other people were present when I used the sword, including the "swordee." One of these was my brother, Tony, with whom I have barely discussed the incident over the intervening 18 years. I'll let him tell the story in his own words. You can compare it to my account found in my first book. People who view or participate in the same situation from various perspectives may come away with compatible recollections, but the little things they remember are often unique.

Before I call my brother, let me set the stage. The following incident happened on a summer afternoon in 1981 in the basement of a ranch house cut into the top of a wooded hillside. The basement faced the yard, which leveled off to a field and thick stand of mixed scrub and timber. Four 17- and 18-year-old males were gathered in the tiled gameroom of the club basement, with a pool table as the centerpiece.

The four characters in order of appearance were as follows:

- Howard, nicknamed Hug, a kind, compassionate, but brooding son of a reformed brawler who had become an evangelical Christian. He stood 5-11 and weighed in at a soft 220. Howard had just showed up, apparently intending to witness to his Godless friends yet again.
- My brother Tony, nicknamed Tango for his cockiness and belligerent nature on the soccer field. Tony was a superb natural athlete whose athletic career and military service as a paratrooper were hampered by his unusually small size. These hard facts meshed with his natural charisma and high intelligence to form a Napoleon complex of the highest order. Tony was just getting out of bed.
- Rick, nicknamed Sick Rick for various expensive driving stunts

and for doing such things as mailing a 12-foot python to his ex-girlfriend. Sick Rick was a big, muscular atheist and my best friend, who had recently given up his martial arts study for the study of altered mental states, under the tutelage of a local marijuana vendor. Rick was just hanging out at our dad's place, enjoying a modified state of being.

• Jim (that would be me), a savage and tenacious brawler, and mediocre athlete. Since quitting school on my 16th birthday, I had basically been living in the woods and practicing martial arts. I was intensely antisocial, fought with my brother periodically, and lived by a harsh self-imposed code of honor that was basically derived from reading Conan and Tarzan stories. I had recently given up my martial arts study for the study of applied lust, under the tutelage of a well-equipped 27-year-old divorcee. I was on the phone scheduling a lesson with my instructor as Howard walked through the door.

Now, you say, with these four well-adjusted young men in one room, how could anything go amiss? Let Tony recount the ways.

CONAN'S LITTLE BROTHER

Incident #19-14 & 15
Time of occurrence: day
Duration: 15–20 seconds
Perspective: defender/eyewitness

"I remember Howard coming up that day, and he had brought a Christian music tape and started playing the music. [Author's note: I recall Tony's taking it out and putting in AC/DC's *Back in Black*, but Tony doesn't.) I think you were in the back. [They were making so much noise that I couldn't hear over the phone, so I stepped into the TV room.]

"I started bashing his music: 'Sounds like queers rattling dildos,'—that kind of stuff. I was really getting to him. I must have hit a nerve. I sent him off like a rocket. It was so unlike him to attack anybody—uncharacteristic. But all of a sudden you saw his dad in his eyes—that rage.

"The next thing I knew he started pushing. At that point I thought it would blow over—didn't realize the rage. I unfortunately backed into the corner [between the bathroom door and the sliding glass door to the patio]. I do remember seeing Rick sitting there [on the couch on the other side of the bathroom door] and thinking he would step in. I think Rick said something later about thinking I deserved it to a certain point.

"He was pinning me against the wall with his body and slamming in body punches, and I was blocking about 99 percent of them because they were just meat-hook punches. He was in a rage, and I was just looking at his hands. He never caught me in the head and kept pressing me against the wall. I think his punches were holding me up for a while, and the fact that he wasn't hurting me was really pissing him off.

"The initial reaction was 'oh, shit!'— survival and protection. I was 17, between 90 and 100 pounds—I was only 100 when I graduated and went into the army. Howard was over 200 pounds. I wasn't going to fight much after backing into the corner—that was a mistake— and there was no plan B.

"This is when he grabbed me by the neck. I guess this is when we pissed you off 'cause you were setting up a date. [I remember hearing Tony gasp along with the sound of his body hitting the panel wall or door.] I don't remember seeing you come out of the back, but I remember seeing the long phone cord. I don't think you said anything then but went to your bedroom for the sword. I never knew why you didn't just pull him off. [I just wanted Howard to leave so I could get on with my phone conversation. I didn't think Howard thought he could take me to begin with, so I figured showing the big blade would settle things in a hurry. I, too, had no plan B.]

My plan was to cover, and it would blow over. Then he grabbed me by the throat, picked me up, and started choking me. And when I noticed that Rick wasn't moving I remember thinking, 'Oh, shit, this is it; it's all over!'

"Then you came out of the bedroom by the corner of the pool table with the sword—I wanted some help, but I thought that was a little much—and told him to leave. I think the sword got his attention. He dropped me, and I was trying to recover in the corner while you came around the pool table in front of my bedroom—the pool table was between you guys at first—and then you stood in front of the other sliding glass door and told him to leave, to get out.

"I was behind him, you guys were a few steps apart, and Howard says, 'Jim, don't try that shit with the sword.'[I did not recall this statement until Tony related it to me. But when I heard it I remembered how angry I felt when Howard said that. I felt like I had given him a chance to walk without taking a beating, or backing down from a fair fight.]

"Then he took a step or two toward you. I thought he was going to try and grab the sword; then I saw it come down. I didn't see where it hit him [left forearm]; I was still catching my breath. Then there was a hesitation—almost like a slow motion. I didn't know he had been hit until I saw the blood spurting—it shot! That was another one of those 'oh, shit!' moments.

"Howard went outside. I don't remember what he or you said or what you did. But I remember you ended up hiding out at Donnie's place. Rick starting wiping up the blood, cleaning the place up, hiding your weapons. He took the sword and threw it out in the field. That's about when Dad came home from work and found Howard at the top of the driveway or up the road and took him to the hospital.

Before you and Dad got back it was crazy. Howard's father came up with Mr. Giovanni. Thank God, Mr. Giovanni was there. Howard's dad had that same look of rage. He said, 'Howard's a lot bigger than you. Why aren't you marked up.'

"I told them that he hit me in the body. So they lifted up my shirt and looked at the welts. They were still red and hadn't bruised up yet. The next thing I remember we were all in the basement, sitting around the pool table filling out statements. And they made Rick go get the sword."

Sorry, Dad. That must have been a hell of a thing to come home to after working a 90-hour week.

In general, Tony saw more and heard less than I did. He had almost no knowledge of the actual stroke and resulting injury. Neither one of us remembers exactly what I did after Howard left, having growled to me that he would "be back." After delivering the diagonal down stroke, having trouble getting it out of his forearm (the moment of hesitation Tony noted), and hearing his promise to return (with his deer rifle, I assumed), the next thing I remember was running through the woods to a friend's house.

Experiences like the one above help me analyze the necessarily partial accounts I receive from witnesses of, and participants in, such acts. More important, it reminds me how dangerous an older teenage male is. A high percentage of anyone's potential attackers—especially those armed and in groups—fall into that age range. If I had to go back in time and fight my 18-year-old self, the adult would be the underdog, despite the years of training and experience. At that age, aggressive males have few of the inhibitions that have been ingrained into us as committed adults.

No wonder 18 is the average age at which warrior societies and modern military establishments recruit their killers.

LES COMES BACK

Incident #52-25
Time of occurrence: seconds
Duration: 15–20 seconds
Perspective: first-person aggressor

When Owen hit Les in the small of the back with a throw of his folding knife, Les was on his way to get a machete he used for yard work from the next room.

Les returned with the machete, cornered Owen, hit him over the collarbone with the back of the blade, punched him in the mouth with his left fist, pressed the front curve of the blade against his belly, and said, "If you flick a nerve I'll put this right through ya."

Owen and Les were both arrested for their part in this and incident on pages 80–81.

A BURGLAR'S NIGHTMARE

Incident #41-02
Time of occurrence: night
Duration: minutes
Perspective: secondhand account related by swordsman's business associate

A big-time coke dealer came upon a burglary in process as he returned home. He had plenty of firepower on hand but wanted to teach this guy a lesson. He grabbed an unusually sharp, high-grade steel machete and hamstrung the burglar. He then called the police and continued the butcher job, slashing the hapless burglar about a dozen times and getting blood all over everything.

The cops claimed probable cause, searched the

room where the butcher work was done, and found 2 kilos. He appears to have done more time on the assault-with-a-deadly-weapon charge than on the possession-with-intent charge.

I DON'T THINK SO

Incident #15-07
Time of occurrence: night
Duration: seconds
Perspective: eyewitness

Tyrell was a short, fat, high-volume, high-profile drug dealer who was working his way into distribution and expanding his territory into a white-trash enclave of the city, where, believe it or not, there is little or no gun violence throughout the year. The local drug merchants—including Tyrell—were smart enough to avoid "cappings," because bullets brought police and guns brought stiffer sentences. None of the local clientele—being crackheads and heroin addicts—had guns, so fists, bats, and blades were adequate for low-level enforcement.

That's where Raphael came in. He didn't use or move dope, but if you bought him dinner every night, paid his cab fare, lavished expensive martial arts equipment on him, and talked about setting up a martial arts school with him as the master, you could count on him providing muscle when you were in deep or when he happened to be around.

One cold wintry night, not long after Raphael had sunk a tiger claw into the soft flesh of one of Tyrell's antagonists, three locals showed up at the crib. The talk recently had been that Tyrell was nothing without Raphael, and the leader of this group was calling out Tyrell for a fight. Tyrell accepted the challenge only to have the dope fiend pull "a big

Rambo knife." Tyrell ducked inside and returned with a katana in the ready. The dope fiends scattered into the night.

I GOT SOMETHING FOR YOU

Incident #01-23
Time of occurrence: night
Duration: 10–15 seconds
Perspective: first-person defender

One fine evening, Tyrell and Raphael were cruising for chicks after a kung-fu tournament when "two big, dumb whiteboys in a pickup" began threatening and tailgating Tyrell, who pulled over and challenged the white guys to a fight. As the two parties emerged from their respective vehicles, one of the white guys produced a pipe. This inspired Raphael—who still had his competition gear in Tyrell's car—to draw his Chinese broadsword. By the time he deployed the blade and put it in the lead, the whiteboys were on their way back to Bumpkinville.

A NIGHT OF COLUMBUS

Incident #13-17
Time of occurrence: night
Duration: seconds
Perspective: first-person defender

Mack was a kindhearted mechanic and deliveryman who was proud to belong to the local chapter of the Knights of Columbus. Well into his 60s, he sat one Friday night polishing his saber for a Saturday morning event.

A knock on the door startled him since he was

expecting no guests and his daughter had a key. He opened the front door with his left hand, the blade held low, point up and forward. He was greeted by the shocked, bug-eyed young man who was obviously intending a home invasion. The punk stood frozen in apparent terror, his right hand in his front pocket, until Mack said, "Can I help you?"

The punk stammered and then blurted, "No, sir, wrong place," and ran down the street. Mack was taken aback by the incident and was very glad that he had forgotten to put his sword down on the coffee table before answering the door, which was normally his habit.

HARVEY THE HACKER

Incident #13-35
Time of occurrence: night
Duration: 1 second
Perspective: eyewitness

Harvey, a physically unimposing individual, left Taffy's Pub in a huff following an argument with Ed, a larger man. Harvey returned with a sickle, came up behind Ed seated on a barstool, and swung the blade at his head or neck [unclear which]. The blow glanced off the top of Ed's head, and Harvey ran.

The sickle cut off the top of Ed's scalp, with the result that the scalp began to peel away on all sides. As the barmaid called 911, one patron held Ed steady on the stool while another held Ed's scalp together.

Harvey, who is generally disliked and considered crazy, did three years and is now patronizing the bars in that neighborhood again. Taffy's has long since closed, and it's not known whether or not Ed needed extensive medical treatment.

Impressive-looking Asian imports of this variety are the most common sword-type weapons out there. Most of these blades are made of brittle knife steel, not flexible sword steel, and are actually giant knives. They wouldn't rate as serviceable blade-to-blade battlefield weapons.

IT'S MY PARTY!

Incident #48-10
Time of occurrence: night
Duration: seconds
Perspective: secondhand account related by swordsman's neighbor

"This idiot, the one on the news with the sword, lived up the road from me in Carney. Well, he threw this party, and for some stupid reason—you can bet it was a stupid reason—brings this samurai sword downstairs and cuts this other guy's head off. Of course, he's drunk, a real weenie, and white—and therefore scared to death of prison—so he runs off into the woods and hides until the cops get him. Oh, well, what can you say? Jerks will be jerks."

ON THE EDGE

I have already discussed my reasoning for not including the ax, hatchet, and shovel as edged weapons. Had they been included as such they would have fallen into the sword category. There is one incident in which a shovel was used with the intent of cutting, but its edge was too dull to cut. I have not added that incident to the statistical analysis of sword use found at the end of this chapter, but I will present the encounter here because it illustrates how tools often come to be used as weapons and how people pick up on blade use postures.

The protagonist in this story is Duncan, whom you earlier met as a boy. Duncan is in his mid- or late 30s and occupies the number-four slot on my list of 20 not to fight. Only Russel, Bubba Crank, and Mumblejack—all career felons—are to be more feared in personal combat.

Duncan stands 6 feet 2 inches and fluctuates between 220 and 240 pounds. He has piercing—almost demonic—eyes; sports a shaved head or crewcut; and has a short, coarse beard that grows nearly to his eyes. He is not a trained fighter, has a great sense of humor, and, most ominously, is highly intelligent.

Duncan has his own construction business but makes most of his money working as a personal bodyguard for four exotic dancers. "A lot of bachelor parties: one-girl shows, two-girl shows, three-girl shows. My purpose is basically intimidation, making a presence. Everybody wants my job."

Not everybody. I know one large karate black belt who escorted a stripper to a bachelor party and later confided to me that it was the most intimidating situation he had ever been in, and he seriously doubted his ability to protect the young lady against a crowd of drunken jocks. Such doubts are not part of Duncan's mind-set. To him, the rest of the men in the world are nothing but potential victims waiting to screw up. According to "Crazy" Steve Newman, a large accomplished brawler in his own right, "that boy [Duncan] is crazy! I'd never fight him with my bare hands."

BLACK & BROWN WITH A BAD ATTITUDE

Incident #52-29 & 30
Time of occurrence: night
Duration: minutes
Perspective: first-person aggressor

"This was during the blizzard. I came home and parked in a clear spot near my house. There was no chair or anything there. When I came back out, someone had pulled their car so close behind that I would back into them, had put snow under my rear wheels, and had left a letter on the windshield saying what they thought of me. They made the mistake of putting their address on it.

"I banged on the door until this guy—smaller than me—came to the door with his dog. He was talking shit, and the dog was growling. A rottweiler, black and brown with a bad attitude, just like its owner. I spit in the dog's face and said, 'Let it go!' He put the dog back inside and came out with one of those car clubs. He was running his mouth, and he kept it up. A real genius, waving this car club around.

"A friend and I began digging my car out with shovels, and this guy keeps hollering, and just won't let up. He's hovering over my shoulder and won't let it go. There's nothing more irritating than someone talking shit while you're trying to work. So I tried to cut the bottom of his face off—the jawbone—with the shovel. It was a real good shot, sent him flying, and then he ran. I missed the jaw. When he pulled his shirt up for the cops there was a nice welt from the left collarbone running diagonally to the right chest.

"He runs for the trunk of his car, yelling that he's going to get his gun and shoot me. So I followed him and broke the key off in the trunk lock. That's when his wife came outside. She had this 13-inch butcher knife hiding up her sleeve, and she pulls it out. I don't remember how she held it . . . like she was cutting a cake.

"I didn't hit her. I should have, but she ran inside when the cops came. The cops came and put us both in the truck. We both went to jail. I told the cops he hit me. He hadn't. You always say the other guy hit you. That's good enough to get you thrown out of court—and it was.

"His wife tried suing me for a million dollars. A million dollars. She ran right to the hospital and tried to say I hit her with the car. I should have. She was right in front of me with the knife. Just like a parasite jumping on the back of a bus after a wreck."

CONCLUSION

Although the sword retains great potential as a recreational tool and home-defense weapon, it has no other practical purpose and seems to draw a disproportionate level of legal attention to the user. The weapon itself is not often used by those who have any skill, and various types of big blades do not appear to be used differently than others. I have documented one case of an unarmed drunk and his youngest son disarming the eldest son, also drunk, who attempted to split his father down the middle during a domestic fracas. (This incident is not included in this book.) The untrained typically use the sword as if it were a stick rather than as a large knife.

12 SWORD DEPLOYMENTS
(PERCENTAGES)

			SWORDSMAN					
Weapon	**Show**	**Warn**	**Slash**	**Lead**	**Ready**	**Drunk**	**Legal**	**Medical**
Sword	42	8	50	17	83	58	50	8

Antagonist	**Drunk**	**Group**	**Armed**	**KO'd**	**Medical**	**Legal**	**Death**
Aggressor	33	50	50	-	33	-	-
Defender	67	-	-	-	50	-	17

CHAPTER 9

Dressed to Kill

Practical Blade-Related Survival Attire and Accessories

The leatha jacket saved me. The knife —it was one a those hook knives—cut through the leatha, my shirt, en me, and got stuck. I busted 'im then and went upside a telephone pole— one of those creosote kind with the splinters—with his face: wore his punk ass out. I like to kill that muthafuca.

—Duke

Duke attributed his survival in the above incident to his leather jacket. I have talked to a others who have used or witnessed the use of a coat, jacket, or smock during the course of a blade encounter. In all cases the use was successful and decisive.

Three mornings ago, on my way home from work, I was attacked by two stray male dogs. I dispersed them easily with the aid of a handheld flannel jacket that I flicked in the face of the alpha male while I tried to score a stomp on the lead leg of the beta. They soon decided that a plunge into speeding rush-hour traffic was preferable to any more time on the blacktop with me.

From avoiding a potentially infectious bite during a dog dispersal to surviving a knife stroke, the jacket is tops.

The gaucho wrapped his poncho on his left arm to use it as a shield and flourished his falcon, or knife, with a sword-like blade and a guard to the handle.

—W.H. Hudson on mid-19th century duels between Argentine frontiersmen

131

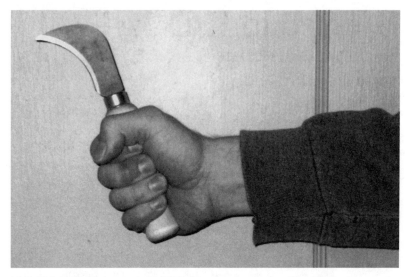

This $7 hook knife is a common, light construction tool used to cut linoleum and carpet. Technically, it could qualify as a razor. But it is mounted, used, and regarded by those who defend against it as a knife. All three of the known uses of this tool as a weapon were single, inward lateral cuts to the left torso. In each case, the knife was held out to the side in the grip depicted in this photo.

FOR THE LATIN KINGS

Incident #48-08
Time of occurrence: night
Duration: 10–12 seconds
Perspective: eyewitness

It was a cold autumn night in Chicago when the Latin Kings, the dominant Hispanic gang, met the Cherry Busters, a mixed gang with a strong Italian membership, to settle a turf dispute. This figured to be a minor skirmish between some of the younger members of the respective gangs. The turf battle went down in the parking lot of a high school near the corner of 48th and Woolcott.

Raphael's older brother, Julio, was not a King but had accompanied the younger boys to the meeting nonetheless. He had recently returned from a long visit to Puerto Rico and was apparently looking out for his little brother. Raphael was standing behind Julio for the duration of Julio's confrontation with an older member of the Cherry Busters.

As the gangs came together, Julio was approached and insulted by a Cherry Buster named Coz. The gangs stopped and stood their ground as Coz "talked shit" to Julio, who never said a word. As Coz was "disrespecting" him, Julio took off his light leather jacket, draped it over his left forearm, wrapped it around, and tied off the sleeves in a knot with his teeth.

As Coz continued to escalate his one-sided war of words, Julio reached into his back pants pocket with his right hand and deployed his 5-inch side-locking switchblade (the very same switchblade used by Raphael in Chapter 1), concealing it behind his leg.

As Coz stepped closer with his foul mouth and disrespectful gestures, Julio feinted to his face with the jacketed hand. Coz parried and skipped back, narrowly avoiding a lunging thrust (from the ready) of the switchblade.

Without hesitation, Julio shifted his attack to a pronated (knuckles up, palm down) lead lunge, which arched over Coz's guard and plunged downward to the hilt into the solar plexus.

Coz jumped back, reached into the pocket of his open jacket, deployed a hooked lock blade out to the side with his right hand, and made an inward cut.

"Somebody said, '*Tiene filete!*' (He's got a blade!) But he let my brother see it. As soon as he snapped it out, Julio was on him."

Julio stepped in to the left, "checked the blade"

with his jacketed arm, and scored with a vicious arching stab from the ready, which scored somewhere below the ribs.

Julio recovered, covered with his left "like a boxer," checked Coz's leading backhand stroke with the jacket (an inward parry), and slashed backhanded from an inside ready (covered by the left) into and across the liver, the blade cutting diagonally up into the left breast (heart area).

Coz stepped back, dropped his knife, doubled up, grabbed his gut, and coughed. Two of his boys grabbed him and pulled him back as the other Cherry Busters began pulling out their belts. Picking up on this development, Raphael yelled, "Kings, move in!" The Cherry Busters dispersed, with their wounded.

Of course, there was no resulting legal action. (By now you should know better than to ask that question.) Raphael and I went over this entire sequence five times in his living room. By the look in his eyes as he recounted his brother's action, it was apparent that he had been awed by the grace and decisiveness of his least violent brother. He said that his brother later confided that he had learned the art of the blade from their uncle in Puerto Rico. When I asked Raphael to summarize the fight, this is what he said:

"My brother knew this mutherfucker and that they were going to go. The stupid idiot blew his chance when he ran off at the mouth while Julio was preparing for battle. Julio was pacing like a tiger. You could see it. The way I see it, Coz never had a chance."

Having witnessed as a boy his brother's tactics of fighting with the jacket on his arm would pay big dividends for Raphael 23 years later on the Southeast Baltimore waterfront. . . .

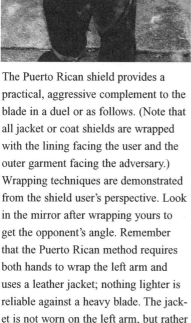

The Puerto Rican shield provides a practical, aggressive complement to the blade in a duel or as follows. (Note that all jacket or coat shields are wrapped with the lining facing the user and the outer garment facing the adversary.) Wrapping techniques are demonstrated from the shield user's perspective. Look in the mirror after wrapping yours to get the opponent's angle. Remember that the Puerto Rican method requires both hands to wrap the left arm and uses a leather jacket; nothing lighter is reliable against a heavy blade. The jacket is not worn on the left arm, but rather wrapped around it. (Photo by Khristopher Kramer.)

Step 1: Grab the sleeve above the cuff and wrap the back of the hand and then over the wrist while you fade right. From here, you can use it as a blinder or blade catcher, or you can progress to step 2.

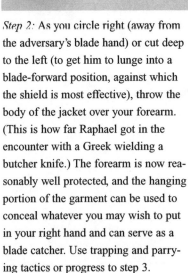

Step 2: As you circle right (away from the adversary's blade hand) or cut deep to the left (to get him to lunge into a blade-forward position, against which the shield is most effective), throw the body of the jacket over your forearm. (This is how far Raphael got in the encounter with a Greek wielding a butcher knife.) The forearm is now reasonably well protected, and the hanging portion of the garment can be used to conceal whatever you may wish to put in your right hand and can serve as a blade catcher. Use trapping and parrying tactics or progress to step 3.

Step 3: While shuffle-stepping or otherwise feinting with your feet, grab the hanging right sleeve and wrap it around the back of the left hand and grab the sleeve below the cuff with your left. Hook the hanging tail of the jacket with the sleeve as you wrap it so as to draw the tail up over the upper forearm. You now have a full-fledged shield with which you can block or even catch stabs. (Before his fight against Coz, Julio not only had time to do a full wrap, but even knotted the sleeves over his wrist, tying them off with his teeth.)

HANGING WITH CUZ

Incident #13-02
Time of occurrence: day
Duration: 10–12 seconds
Perspective: first-person aggressor

Raphael had stopped by Tyrell's new crib in response to a phone call from Tyrell requesting help with "a problem." The problem turned out to be three Greeks who couldn't handle Raphael.

After putting two of Tyrell's antagonists out of action, Raphael faced the third, who was advancing with a butcher knife. Raphael backed up as he slipped out of his jacket and wrapped it over his left forearm. As the knifer hesitated and stalled in a square stance, Raphael stepped in, deflecting a side-arm slash with the jacketed arm, as he attacked the knifer's right elbow with an underhanded slap, ejecting the blade. He flowed immediately into a heel-palm to the chest, sending the knifer through a storefront window. Tyrell and Raphael were not present when the cops showed up 10 minutes later.

THE LUCKY LEGEND

Incident #53-21
Time of occurrence: night
Duration: 5 seconds
Perspective: secondhand account from the son of Lucky's cousin

Lucky was a stocky Italian streetfighter from Philadelphia, who was called on to fight in a gang-related blade challenge. He wore a thick winter coat wrapped over his left arm and charged in "like a bull," stabbing from the ready with an underhand

The Italian shield. The Italian method of using a coat as a shield requires a thigh- or ankle-length coat. It can be deployed with the left arm while the right hand is busy drawing a weapon. (The coat is always worn on the shield arm.) Gloves are recommended. This method is suitable for dueling, though it is less versatile than the Puerto Rican method. The Italian shield is primarily a hitter's gambit used to approach and then to blind or pin the unarmed target of a stabbing.

The drape. Three paces from his target, the knifer shrugs his right arm out of his trench coat as he holds out his left arm, which becomes a curtain hanger. The coat falls nearly to the floor, concealing his knife hand as the blade is drawn. He takes a step forward with a cross-arm guard. Whip the coat across the target's line of sight or drape it over his head on the second step. On the third step, grab the target and stab and stab and stab. . . . The drape is most effective (for cover and defense, not stabbing) with the hand held in the coat pocket, as shown.

The whip. To use as a defensive tactic against an aggressor, weave the arm back under the body of the coat, resulting in a triple layer of forearm protection and a long twisted coattail, which can be used to lash across the attacker's face with a backhand motion. (This is a jarring blow with an oilskin.)

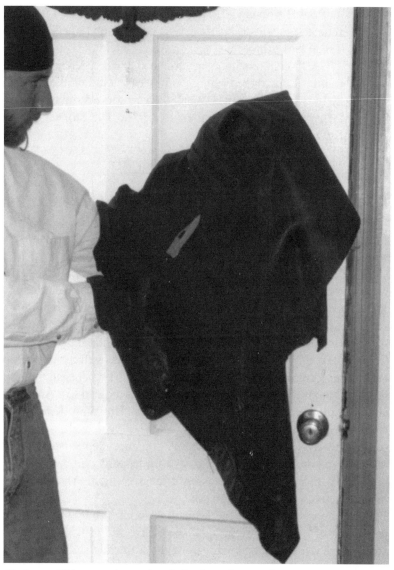

The hanger. If time permits—as in a duel—throw the coattail once more over the forearm, providing five layers of protection, and then use it as a means of crowding the opponent. There is sill enough of a tail to whip with, and it can be easily unwound to suffocate or muffle the cries of a mounted knifer. If you can catch a stab with the hanger, immediately twist to your left to wrench the blade from your adversary's hand.

motion. His opponent, caught trying to circle from a square stance, was stabbed, bowled over, and abandoned by his brothers.

Although this incident produced an emergency-room patient, there were no witnesses (including the victim) willing to finger Lucky. There was a similar lack of future blade challenges for Lucky: a one-fight legend.

THE OLDEST SHIELD

Using a coat, leather jacket, smock, or a spare shirt to defend against a blade is certainly a practice as old as the blade itself. It would only be natural for the prehistoric hunter to armor himself with the skin of his prey.

The most feared modern shield fighter was the Zulu warrior, whose cowhide shield was an integral component in some of the most successful close-quarter fighting tactics ever employed by lightly armed and unarmored men. (Depending on the authority, the Modern Age is defined as beginning either 1453 A.D. with the capture of Constantinople by the Ottoman Turks or 1492 A.D. with the discovery of a future resort by an Italian confidence man who believed that the Earth was as small as Mars. The Zulu nation was molded like "so much clay" beginning in 1816, by Shaka, aka "He Who Kills with Afflictions." Nice guy.)

Hannibal's Numidian light cavalry —the most dependable troops of their kind during the Punic Wars—wore leopard skin draped over their left arms, which served as an offensive shield. The shield is most effective when used aggressively.

The modern picture of the Roman period is strongly colored by the drama of gladiators fighting to the death, one of whom is often armed with the trident and net: essentially a flexible shield.

During the Renaissance (from the 15th through the 17th centuries in Europe), the cloak was often relied upon by swordsmen. And still later, the cane-wielding nobleman of the 19th century was said to rely on his cape as a shield and blinder.

Since childhood, I have studied the use of the flexible shield and have carried one religiously since 1985. 1 have used it as a defensive weapon against a German police dog and as an offensive weapon against a large kung-fu fighter. In recent years I have interviewed people who have used a jacket —or have seen the jacket used—as an offensive or defensive weapon. I have taken this information, synthesized it with my practical experience, and tested it in knife sparring matches with Chuck Goetz—who recently blinded me during a morning scrimmage on a deserted ballcourt. The following is my understanding of the most practical and effective uses of the flexible shield, in the context of our current social climate.

MY BEST INANIMATE FRIEND

The crew jacket is a lined, quilted flannel shirt, not as reliable or durable as a leather jacket, but is superior to a windbreaker, has multiple practical uses (such as being worn as a trench coat liner), and is cheap enough to be easily replaced by a lowly working stiff like the author. The waist wrap is a practical carry option, although it will earn you a citation from the fashion police.

BLINDING AND BLADE-CATCHING TACTICS

Head Drape
The head drape is difficult to execute. But using an opponent's head for a coat rack for even a second will give you a good shot at taking him down or out, or running away.

Face Whip
The face whip is a highly effective, low-commitment tactic much like the jab in boxing. Snap it like a towel at the eyes.

Tangle
The tangle is a counterthrusting tactic. Draw a lead-hand thrust to your gut. As you draw-step to the outside of your opponent's knife hand, whip the (preferably pretwirled) jacket down over his elbow. With practice you can get a 1- second wrap on every third try. If you do, stab him in the neck or armpit. If unarmed, tackle him. Chances

Illustrated use of the crew jacket, denim jacket, or lined flannel shirt. The light jacket should be held in the hand and used as a blinder and blade catcher, or "throw-wrapped" like the Italian hanger. Don't wear the sleeve; it's not heavy enough.

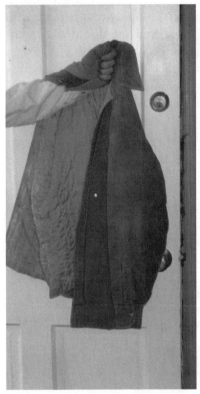 

The carry. For the first wrap from the carry, hold the jacket by the collar so that the back of your hand will be covered on the first wrap. Make the hanger with the second and third wrap on the move. A draw step will actually aid the twirling action of throwing the jacket over the forearm. You can have a full wrap in less than 2 seconds and be three paces off the knifer's intended mark.

The waist wrap. The second most accessible carry option is the waist wrap. Wearing the jacket around the waist will help protect the abdominal area and kidneys and allow you to deploy with either hand. Tie the sleeves in a loose knot in front of the right hip. The attack will come from the left, so you don't want to be fumbling around over there.

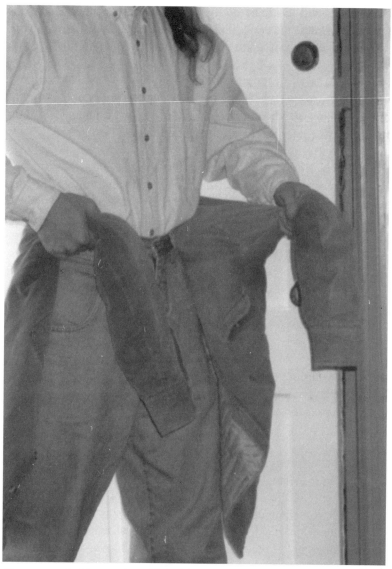

The gut curtain. Unwrapping with both hands as you get the hell off the mark causes enough tension to make a temporary curtain against low stabs to the left and center and allows you to whip the jacket at your antagonist's eyes and knife with either hand. These tactics are useless without mobility.

are that this will just hang up his hand for a half-second, which may give you a shot at slashing his forearm as he pulls out. Combine this with the face whip. It is not something you can just go for.

Pass and Slash

For the pass and slash, arc the jacket across your opponent's line of sight with a backhand as you slash low with a forehand. I score a lot of thrusts (sparring) by shifting into the lead from here.

Toss and Rush

To perform the toss and rush, you explode and throw the balled jacket into your opponent's face as you charge. If you abort, you have given him a shield.

WRAPPED-ARM TACTICS

Parry

Parry—never block against the blade—with the wrapped arm. A tightly rolled newspaper is an excellent complement.

Pinning and Jawing

Once you pin your opponent, smashing and bashing puts you at less risk than striking with the free hand. Unless, of course, you happen to have a screwdriver in your back pocket.

Jacket Grab

For the jacket grab, use the loosely wrapped hand to grab your opponent's knife hand. Experimentation has shown this to be a viable approach only if the knifer has less fighting ability than his opponent. I would recommend this tactic for use only against women and weak males who lead with the blade. After you have scored with a jacket grab or any of the wrapped-arm tactics, a knee or ankle stomp is highly recommended.

HISTORICAL NOTES

The shield was more important to, and used more *aggressively* by, the Zulu warrior than any other hand-to-hand fighting man in history. Any comprehensive study of the Zulu nation, Shaka Zulu, and the struggles among the Zulus and the Boers and the British in South Africa should discuss the cultural conditioning and mind-set of the aggressive shield and blade fighter. Effective shield use requires the same mental, emotional, and physical attributes as does effective blade use.

Not only did Shaka (imagine a cross between Adolph Hitler, Michael Jordan, and Lestat, the vampire in Anne Rice's novels) revolutionize the use of the shield, he reinvented the native blade, transforming the *assegai*, a throwing weapon, into the *iklwa*, a stabbing weapon. The term *iklwa* is an imitation of the sucking sound made when the wide blade is withdrawn from the body. As his victim slid off his blade Shaka would yell, "*Ngadla* (I have eaten)!"

Poking around in the library may seem like a weakling's solution to acquiring blade knowledge. But there are so few articulate modern humans equipped with firsthand knowledge of blade use that viewing the real blade fighters of the past through the clear lens provided by a first-class historical writer—not necessarily a historian—is worth a read.

The standard work on the Zulus is Donald R. Morris' *The Washing of the Spears: The Rise and Fall of the Zulu Nation* (New York: Simon and Schuster, 1965).

WORDS OF WISDOM BORN OF EXPERIENCE

As Raphael put it:

"If anybody comes after you with a knife, and you have a jacket—even if it's just a windbreaker—deal with it. Be quick. You don't have much time.

"The worn jacket is better than nothing but inferior to the jacket on the arm. With the jacket on the arm or in the hand, you have an offensive tool. Action beats reaction. Take it to him.

"Leather is the best. Heavy leather turns a blade well. However, this [lifts a lid off an aluminum trash can] is the ultimate street shield. In Chicago we used to cut off the rim and sharpen the edge.

I would use this with the shaft of a rake [picks up rake and makes stomping motion above tool head] or any long handle [points to shovel] against the blade.

"The staff is used best by the Chinese—dragon-pole style. The Japanese styles have no concept of the shield. The Chinese systems recognize the shield. The shield is a weapon."

CHAPTER 10

Getting Stuck in the Grapple

Blades and Shanks in the Grapple

I would totally be into wrestling, except for the fact that your ears'll look like pussy lips. Why don't they crop 'em, like you do with a pit bull?

—Rick Wayne

SUZY

Incident #28-10
Time of occurrence: night
Duration: seconds
Perspective: first-person defender

Suzy, a young restaurant manager, was crossing a downtown parking lot when she was grabbed from behind by a small, wiry man—much stronger than she—who held a knife to her throat and demanded her money. She froze in terror, and she does not really recall the details of what happened next. The mugger was apparently spooked by a group of people walking to their car, and he fled.

KAZIA

Incident #53-23
Time of occurrence: day
Duration: 10 seconds to a minute
Perspective: secondhand account related by Kazia's Aunt Carol

Kazia and a rival teenaged girl got into a sidewalk dispute that became a fight and soon turned into a "clinch-and-claw" affair. The other girl drew a box cutter and sliced Kazia from the left temple, through the left eye, and down across the cheek to the corner of her mouth. The slicer was hauled into juvenile court and reprimanded.

GRAPPLING

Of 1,000 acts of violence, 382 involved, or resulted in, grappling tactics. Grapples are defined as clinches (both parties remain upright), throws (one party remains upright), and floor fights.

This is probably going to be the most controversial aspect of my work. Virtually every self-defense expert—including some highly respected real fighters—make such statements as "90 percent of all fights go to the ground" or "virtually all fights result in grappling."

In some cases, you are hearing the advice of a bouncer who has witnessed countless half-fights between drunks, which tend to occur indoors and in crowded circumstances. In at least one case such advice comes from a powerful judoku (judo practitioner) who prefers to grapple and, because he always faces less skilled and less experienced antagonists, tends to get things his way.

In at least three cases this advice has been given by men who typically finish fights at punching range but who believe themselves to be the exception, the rule being that most fights end in grappling.

Then there are the neglected considerations: attacks and weapons that tend to complement one another. Most fighters, even self-defense teachers, only consider violence from the competitive perspective of the challenge, contest, or "match fight." In part, our misunderstanding of grappling in real situations is a semantic one. Let's look at some hard statistics:

- Thirty-eight percent of violence involves grappling. That is a grab of any kind by the defender or aggressor and does not include pushing, shoving, and "bulldozing."
- Twenty-four percent of armed encounters involve grappling. From this statistic one might infer that as many as 50 percent of unarmed confrontations involve grappling. Why grab your victim when you have a howitzer?
- Thirty-seven percent of violence involves weapon use. This reinforces the last point.
- Forty-two percent of grapples are indecisive, compared with 30 percent overall. Now, an aggressor wants a decisive resolution, while a defender is more apt to settle for the indecisive. Since grapples are less decisive and aggressors get their way four times as often as defenders, one would assume (and indeed it is true) that most violence does not involve grappling for the very good reason that most aggressors prefer not to grapple. Does Jimbo really want to be wrasslin' with his opponent, while Joe Bob is whalin' away with that ax handle? Of course not. The violent felon wants to be able to get his licks in, too, like his buddy—which brings us to another predatory trend. . . .
- Twenty-five percent of all aggression is committed by groups. This once again points to the predatory nature of most violence.

Many times, I have heard or read the sales pitch of a grappling master who promotes his art as a more civilized and "personally bonding" activity than kicking and punching. With this I agree. Wrestlers are much more social than boxers. Wrestlers are many times more apt than boxers to engage in team sports. They are more likely to socialize as a group, binge drink together, double-date together, and gang-rape together than are boxers. Wrestlers are also more apt to excel in the business world, particularly in sales.

By now I have certainly miffed the jujutsu and karate stylists who do not like to be compared with wrestlers and boxers any more than they like to be matched up against them. But these are the two basic grappling and striking archetypes in the modern world. No human—not even a prostitute—spends more time in the grapple than a wrestler. Likewise, nobody—not even an abused wife of an alcoholic sadist—is struck with bad intent as often as a boxer.

So when the happy-hugging grappler portrays 90 percent of violence as involving grappling, he is expressing his knowledge that he could technically take anything that stands on two legs to the floor. The basic disconnect comes when one realizes that the violent felon rarely wants to go to the floor. He wants you there under the heels of his Doc Martens. The single glaring exception to this rule is rape, although many of the rapes I have documented occurred with both parties standing.

I will take this one step further by pointing out that most of those who fight do not wish to go to the floor.

- Seventeen percent of trained fighters grappled with their opponents.
- Fifty percent of wrestlers grappled with their opponents! Only half? A lot of them tell me that wrestling ability gives them the luxury of winging away with punches without worrying about going to the floor.
- Fifteen percent of floor fights were between sober adult males, accounting for only 2 percent of violence.
- Thirteen percent of my violent experiences involved grappling. The fact that my experience with grappling is less than that of other trained fighters relates to the fact that I have experienced a higher proportion of armed encounters than is normal for a trained fighter. Trained fighters are less than half as likely as untrained fighters to use a weapon. My small size and the fact that I live in a city make me an exception.

When we discuss grappling we must not automatically assume that the grapple will go to the ground. It probably will not, unless at least one party wants it to.

The longest fight between two adult males occurred in a roadhouse bar of this type. It involved Big Sam, a 6-foot, 6-inch, 260-pound minor-league football player, who was very drunk, and Lance, a 5-foot, 7-inch, 170-pound mercenary and former Navy SEAL, who had just returned from a job in Central America. Coked up at the time, Lance was very rude to Sam's lady friend. The brawl lasted 10 to 15 minutes, featured extensive upright grappling and wall slamming, and ended in a draw because of mutual exhaustion. At no point did the fight go to the floor. Cocaine and alcohol fight to a draw! What a sports headline.

GRAPPLING WITH THE BLADE

There are four contexts in which the blade appears in a grappling situation.

1. Warnings
2. Draws from the grapple
3. Grab-and-stab or grab-and-slice attacks
4. Grappling responses to blade attacks

Warnings

Suzy's ordeal (described at the beginning of this chapter) was a classic case of warning with the blade; the knifer's variation of the gunman's holdup. There are other reasons why such situations develop. Sandy's rescue of Dan in Chapter 6 is an interesting case. The target of such a threat is almost always the throat, though the face of a woman or the wrist of a larger man may also be targeted. If the warning escalates to a knifing, you are looking at a slice, as opposed to the stab or slash.

NO, BUCK YOU!

Incident #52-01
Time of occurrence: night
Duration: over 10 seconds
Perspective: first-person aggressor

Raphael, Jose, and Vega were on leave in Fayetteville, North Carolina. They were coming out of a club called The Flame when they noticed that two GIs were in an altercation with two Lumbee Indians, while three Lumbee girls looked on. The one GI was frozen, and the other was in the grasp of the larger Lumbee, who had a lock blade pressed to his throat.

Jose demanded that the Lumbee release the GI. The Lumbee refused and began to press the blade into the GI's neck. The altercation was apparently over the Lumbee's girl, who was present.

Jose, who was a "NewYorRican" streetfighter, grabbed the girl around the neck, pulled his own Buck lock blade, held the blade under her right breast, and said, "Let him go or I'm going to do to her what you do to him. How bad do you really want your girl? You cut him; I'm gonna cut her."

The Lumbee responded, "I'll cut him."

The girl screamed, and the Lumbee shoved the GI toward Jose and threatened "to shank him."

Jose whispered in the girl's ear, "I ain't gonna hurt you," backed away from the girl, and said, "Go ahead, sweetheart."

The Lumbee—a true idiot—pocketed his blade (?!) and started talking shit to Jose, running his mouth and telling Jose to leave. Jose kept his blade out, and we stepped up.

Jose said, "You want me to leave? You leave!"

"It was what you call a Mexican standoff. We would've killed those Lumbees. Jose could fight, and there was Vega and me," recalled Raphael. "They just didn't want to back down right away in front of their girls. The boy had a 4- to 5-inch pressure cut—the length of the blade—along the left side of the throat. I didn't even know Jose carried a blade until then.

"The girls from Lumberton are nothing but trouble, just looking for GI benefits."

Draws from the Grapple

Talk about an ugly prospect! This is a real hazard for individual security personnel. If shanking you is a ticket to freedom, your opponent will take it. If you apply the grapple, he has the emotional advantage of feeling threatened. Your advantage is the hold. You better make it work.

CATCHING HELL

Incident #50-02
Time of occurrence: night
Duration: minute
Perspective: secondhand account by the knifer's drinking buddy, corroborated by the dead man's friend

David pulled his pickup into the lot of a biker bar and began to load the nicest hog on the lot into his truck. As he was hauling the bike up the ramp, which he kept in the bed of his truck for this exact purpose, six bikers surrounded him and began working him over. He was thrown to the ground and stomped severely. As he made it to his feet, the owner of the bike, who was regarded as a "beautiful and generally nonviolent person," grabbed him for some one-on-one retribution.

Badly beaten, surrounded, and held by a man whose wildly expensive bike he had just tried to steal, David went all out. He deployed his lock blade and sliced the bike owner from the inside of his thigh, just above the knee, up into the solar plexus. This brought a halt to the action as the bike owner's guts began to spill out on the blacktop. His friends and the medics focused their first-aid efforts on keeping his guts inside his body, but he soon died of massive bleeding from the femoral artery, which had been severed below the groin.

David did three years in prison. He currently drinks in a bar a few miles from where he disem-boweled the biker—and a half-mile from where Kane sliced open Russel's massive chest. It is not known if he is still in the business of stealing, but he is thought to still carry a knife and maintain a gen-erally foul disposition. I didn't attempt to interview David, even though I catch the bus across the street from his favorite watering hole. I despise thieves, especially bike, car, and horse thieves.

CLICK!

Incident #05-27
Time of occurrence: day
Duration: 45 seconds
Perspective: first-person aggressor

City supermarket management is a little-known and underappreciated combat specialty. How does an untrained, unarmed customer service specialist make

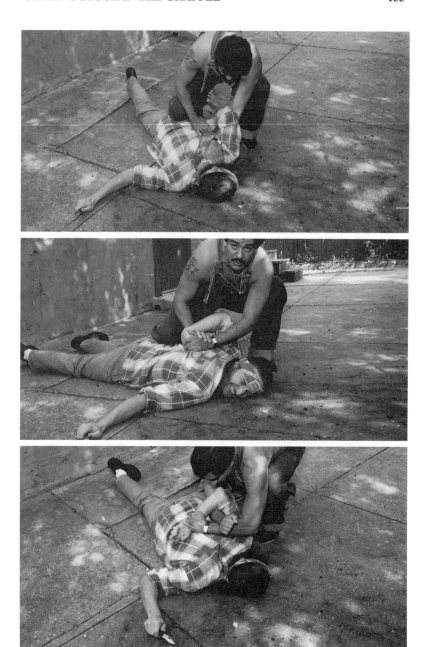

Rich's weak-side knifer takedown.

a smooth transition to the bouncer trade during the last week of every month, when the "food stampers" have depleted their "independence card accounts"?

Well, it doesn't hurt to be a trained grappler. Shoplifter apprehension is an art that focuses on preventing injury to the perp—as much to avoid a blood exchange as a lawsuit.

Rich, a supermarket manager and jujutsu stylist, grabbed a greedy biker wannabe from the left side. The punk drew a folder from his right pants pocket (probably front). Rich did not see the blade. But upon hearing the click of the blade lock, he said to himself, "Oh, shit!" He applied an arm bar and pressed the knifer's chest to the pavement. He had no immediate solution for disarming the punk. But, fortunately, the young men who clerked at that store regarded "shoplifter week" as a sporting event. One of the young scum-chasers was on the case within seconds, stepping on the knifer's wrist and prying the blade loose.

Grab and Stab

NICE BIKE

Incident #02-15
Time of occurrence: day
Duration: 10 seconds to a minute
Perspective: secondhand account by Missy, who testified for the prosecution at the knifer's trial

Lance, a young man, ambushed a teenaged boy on a convenience store parking lot. The boy was pulling in on his bicycle as Lance knocked him off the bike, punched him, and dragged him behind the store; where he mounted the boy and began stabbing and slicing him with a large sheath knife. A police officer intervened, arresting Lance and saving the boy, who was permanently disabled as a result of his injuries.

Lance was released on a low bail. He soon acquired a new Rambo knife and recruited an accomplice, in hopes of furthering his career as a predatory sociopath.

Grappling Responses

The fact that so many knifers are smaller than the unarmed defender begs for a grappling defense. Duncan's battle against Milton in Chapter 7 and Duke's face-smashing of the hook knifer in Chapter 9, as well as some of the successes outlined in Chapter 13, are grappling responses to a blade threat. Of course, the situation that most begs for the grappling response is the draw from the grapple. You already have a handle on the situation. You might as well go with what you've got.

TUCK

Incident #37-12
Time of occurrence: night
Duration: more than 10 seconds
Perspective: first-person aggressor

Tuck, about 6-1 and 350 pounds, was working in a rural biker bar with a dirt floor when an average-sized customer began causing trouble. Tuck grabbed the jerk's left arm to escort him out, which resulted in the jerk's snapping out a lock blade. Tuck immediately cranked the "chicken wing" wrist and elbow lock until the jerk dropped the knife, maintaining the hold until they reached the jerk's vehicle, where he grabbed a tire iron. Tuck cranked up the chicken wing again until everything was cool. "It's a great persuasion device. When you've got it on him he'll do what you say, and say what you want—even about his mom."

DOLL TOSSING

Typically, brawlers who grapple a lot are large, powerful, untrained fighters. These fellows are all over 200 pounds and at least 6 feet tall, giving them a size advantage over their adversaries so great that they are able to throw adult men with the same lack of effort and sophistication demonstrated by a 3-year-old boy hurling his older sister's stuffed animals and dolls at the family pet. In fact, one-handed tosses over vehicles, tables, and walls are common, as are throws of multiple opponents.

Duncan, at 6 foot, 2 inches, 227 pounds, is one of the smallest doll tossers in my study. Duncan has himself been picked up and thrown over a pickup one-handed by a larger, older man. Big Earl, a black longshoreman, is the largest doll tosser, at 7-1 and 410 pounds!

FLOOR FIGHTING

KRAZEE SHANK KILLPOWER

Incident #53-22
Time of occurrence: night
Duration: minutes
Perspective: first-person defender

"When I just got out of the army I was trouble—a hoodlum. In Korea I had been in charge of the motor pool—over 200 vehicles. Back here I was into Black Power. I wasn't all about hurt; I had my gentle ways: poetry, walking and crying all day after my girl got another man. . . .

"I 5-11, 130. Been shot in the face—nose to cheek—carried a knife, and went off easy. If you got somethin'—you carryin'—then trouble find you. 'Cause you got somethin'; you got that attitude. You're not goin' to back down or run. That's how carryin' a knife get you in trouble.

"I carried a steak knife. Between the belt and

the pants in front [motions to left cross-draw position] or back [above the right pocket]. No need for a holder. Those guys with holders have put a sharp edge on their blade. No need to sharpen a steak knife. The teeth do the work.

"Me and this other fella were drinkin' in a house and got to fightin'. A stand-up fight, over what I don't remember. We were drunk. I was young. Long time ago. Long time. He grab a bottle, a wine bottle, I think. He was somewhat bigger than me. I draw the knife like so [back cross draw to lead].

"We go at it and end up fightin' over the knife on the floor. People eventually broke it up, and we both got locked up for assault. I was cut on the arm [points to left forearm] while we was wrestlin'. I kept hold of the knife. I got him cross here [motions with finger from left ear to Adam's apple].

I don't fight or carry a blade no more. No, that askin' for trouble to find you."

INTERVENING WITH THE BLADE

The following constitutes the only known case of the knife's being used as a tool during an altercation. Alain Burrese, author of *Hard-*

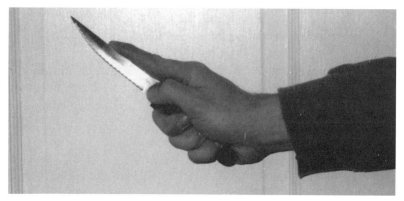

The 99-cent weapon and the preferred fighting grip of Krazee Shank KillPower.

Won Wisdom from the School of Hard Knocks (published by Paladin; out of print), refers to this incident on page 241 of his book. When I interviewed Alain for the Violence Project he gave me the details.

CUTTING LOOSE

Incident #27-21
Time of occurrence: night
Duration: less than a minute
Perspective: first-person aggressor

Alain was working security with Marc "Animal" MacYoung, author of *Knives, Knife Fighting, and Related Hassles* (among other of his Paladin book and video titles), at a club in California. They were intervening in a sidewalk dispute (that had something to do with a parked car) between a civilized customer and an obnoxious drunk.

The drunk had the other man's shirt in a death grip and could not be made to let go. As Alain was restraining the two to the extent possible, Marc pulled his knife and asked the innocent customer if it was OK to cut his shirt. The guy answered in the affirmative (which tells me that the drunk must have been a really unwelcome companion). Marc proceeded to cut him out of his shirt.

This incident absolutely fascinates me. Although knives are tools, they are rarely used as anything but an actual or a potential weapon. The knife used as the "jaws of life" for freeing entangled brawling victims? What a cool idea.

382 GRAPPLES OUT OF 1,000 BY POSTURE
(PERCENTAGES)

Posture	Of All Violence	Of All Grappling	KO	Submit	Choke	3rd Party	Other
Clinch	14	36	14	44	1	30	11
Throw	10	26	34	27	0	18	21
Floor	14	38	16	35	3	33	13

93 BLADE GRAPPLES
(CONSTITUTING 36% OF BLADE ENCOUNTERS)

	POSTURE				SITUATION				RESOLUTION		
Weapon	Clinch	Throw	Floor	Warn	Draw *	Grab **	Resp. ***	KO	Sub. ****	3rd	Other
Razor	64	none	36	none	none	73	27	9	18	27	45
Knife	55	21	24	7	18	37	37	51	21	18	10
Shank	29	29	43	none	none	71	29	71	21	7	-
Sword	50	none	50	none	none	-	100	-	50	50	-

	POSTURE				SITUATION				RESOLUTION		
Lead	50	14	36	none	14	7	79	22	7	57	14
Ready	50	21	29	4	21	50	25	45	24	14	17
Overhand	47	13	40	none	13	60	27	80	7	13	-

NOTES

* Indicates a draw from the grapple.

** Indicates a grappling (grab and stab/slice) attack.

*** Indicates a grappling response to blade/shank attack.

**** Submission.

"Other" denotes exhaustion or by agreement.

A clinch that goes to a throw and to the floor is listed as a floor fight, even if it then goes upright and the choke is applied in the clinch.

LIKELIHOOD OF GRAPPLING BY WEAPON
(PERCENTAGES)

Razor	28
Knife	38
Shank	52
Shank	17

LIKELIHOOD OF GRAPPLING BY POSTURE
(PERCENTAGES)

Lead	16
Knife	47
Shank	38

CHAPTER 11

When You're Food

Dying or Surviving against Long Odds

This Hispanic kid is carrying a loaded dog, which is no different than me carrying my loaded gun. I have to be certified, but any asshole can buy a dog. They'll sue me for everything I own. What am I goin to do, sue this kid for his gold chain?

—Rick Wayne

NICE TATTOO

Incident #02-16
Time of occurrence: day
Duration: less than a minute
Perspective: secondhand account given by Missy, a witness for the prosecution at the knifer's trial

Alvin, a mentally retarded man, was walking along a wooded highway toward his brother's house, when two men, Lance and Joey, approached him asking for a light. As Alvin reached into his pants pocket he was grabbed by Lance while Joey hit him over the head with a bottle.

Lance and Joey strong-armed Alvin into the woods, where Lance drew his sheath knife and went to work on Alvin, who tried to ward off the blade with his hands. He was stabbed through the right hand and thigh, and sliced along the left side and back. When Lance and Joey discovered that Alvin had no money, they took his shirt and belt, thus uncovering his tattoo, which they admired and threatened to cut off. They left Alvin for dead in the woods.

Alvin managed to walk a mile to a gas station for help and lived to testify against his attackers. Lance was sentenced to a total of 15 years for this act and an attack on a boy at the farm store. Joey pleaded guilty to some minor charge. The emergency room doctor was of the opinion that Alvin's unusually tight blue jeans acted as a tourniquet and prevented him from bleeding to death.

GETTING GREASED

Incident #27-03
Time of occurrence: night
Duration: 10–60 seconds
Perspective: related by a fellow Cake

The Cakes were a clique of middle-class athletes and car buffs from the Avonworth section of Pittsburgh. They had a generations-long rivalry with the Greasers, working-class kids from the Northgate neighborhood. Most altercations between the cliques erupted after football games in the parking lots of fast-food joints or at the respective high schools and did not escalate to full combat.

Ben was a Cake who dated a girl from Northgate. One night, Ben and his girl were waiting outside the Bellview Theater when a carload of Greasers threatened him. A short time later a group of Greasers, variously estimated at between four and eight, but most likely five, bum-rushed Ben, took him to the ground, and beat him for less than a minute, while others looked on.

Ben lay unconscious and bleeding, but no one called an ambulance or offered assistance.

After a minute or two he regained consciousness, crawled into his Jeep, drove himself to the hospital, parked the Jeep, and died behind the wheel. Ben had sustained 26 stab wounds to his arms and torso, although his girlfriend never saw a blade. Two Greasers were eventually charged with a crime, and one ended up doing some time. Greasers were known to carry lock blades. There was probably one blade, which had to have been used from the ready since it was not seen.

BEHIND THE STEEL WHEEL

Incident #13-04
Time of occurrence: night
Duration: 20–30 seconds
Perspective: eyewitness

Iggy had just turned left down a dimly lit alley behind a waterfront bar, where he had parked his Harley before nightfall. Before he reached his bike there was a commotion to his rear. As he turned he saw three large men silhouetted in the glow of the street light "push-dragging" a smaller man into the alley.

The three men were to Iggy's right, half-facing him as they held the smaller man with their left hands and beat him with their right fists. One man held the victim's right shoulder, one his collar, and the other his left shoulder, as they punched him in the head, face, and left side of the body. The attackers appeared to be under the influence of cocaine or an amphetamine.

Iggy knew the small man—and knew him to be very drunk—but didn't get involved, for one very good reason.

As the defender was being pummeled and driven down the alley, he reached into his right pants pocket (front or rear is unclear) and deployed a butterfly knife. Iggy could see the blade shine under the street light, but "they didn't see the blade—must'a thought they were gett'n punched."

The defender drove his blade into the left side of the right-most man "at least five times." After every two stokes on the knife-side man, he stabbed the center man once "up the middle of the gut." The stabs sank in beneath the ribs with a smacking thud—the sound of the knifer's fist hitting flesh. Iggy was adamant that the knifer achieved full (that would be about 4 inches) penetration with most of his strokes. The attackers seemed oblivious to the blade and successfully completed their assault, driving the defender to the wall across from Iggy and stuffing him headfirst into an empty trashcan.

When they backed up so that the smaller man was no longer in their shadow, they could see what Iggy had seen. "When he crawled out of the trashcan and stood up, you could see it under the street light. They did a body check and bolted. He kind'a wobbled down the alley."

The above encounter certainly wasn't a typical knife fight. Usually it's one knifer and an unarmed defender. But Iggy's story does illuminate two common aspects of blade use:

1. The blade is often *unseen* and *unfelt.*
2. The blade is not always a decisive factor. The knife-armed defender in this situation did not alter the course of the altercation by seriously injuring two of his attackers!

WHERE IS YOU GOIN'?

Incident #25-15, 25-16
Time of occurrence: night
Duration: 10–20 seconds
Perspective: related by Roger's sister Liz, who
was present at her brother's trial

Roger was crossing the parking lot of a strip mall to purchase a pizza for Liz when a group of seven to twelve black men attacked him. They formed a circle around him as one of the men drew a knife and slashed and stabbed Roger five to ten times. He escaped and went home for his guns: a pistol and a shotgun.

Roger caught up with the knifer and one of the accomplices as the men stepped off the front porch of a house. Roger claimed to have shot four rounds. The police recovered eight shotgun casings from the scene.

The knifer recovered from his wounds well enough to walk into court for Roger's trial, where Roger was sentenced to 15 years, of which he served 11. The knifer was not charged for the stabbing.

WRONG GUY, KID

Incident #36-14
Time of occurrence: night
Duration: seconds
Perspective: related by Billy's sister Pepper, who
was present at his trial and was his confidant

Billy had just left a city convenience store with his entire tax refund in his pocket when he was confronted by a group of black youths who were leaving high school football practice. When the lead boy demanded money, Billy drew his 3 1/2-inch folder and slashed the boy across the left cheek. Billy was arrested, charged, and convicted, ultimately serving three years for assault with a deadly weapon. The cutting "victim" had many witnesses willing to testify to Billy's unprovoked attack.

THE WASTED YOUTH SCREWUP

Incident #13-10
Time of occurrence: night
Duration: less than a minute
Perspective: news report and secondhand account by friend of victim and by a hired blade who refused to take the unfinished job

At age 27 I was working on a supermarket night crew, which consisted of four black men, a young racist skinhead by the name of Tony, Quin, and me.

Quin was an interesting character. By age 19 he had n—had spent a season in a militia compound, had done prison time (becoming affiliated with the Aryan Brotherhood), and had spit in the face of a gunman in a back alley.

Even though he had a visceral dislike for whites who got along with blacks as well as I did, Quin liked me because I spent time with my adopted son. And he had very little respect for Tony, who had built his reputation on his membership in Baltimore Area Skin Heads (a lightweight organization), whose idea of race warfare was beating up black kids who were marching for a charity benefit.

Tony despised me for fraternizing with the blacks on the crew and was highly resentful of my fighting ability. When Tony made the mistake of threatening me one night and I began screaming obscenities into his face—degrading his ancestry, accusing his mother of mating with a mutt dog, and

otherwise goading him to make good on his threat—
Quin looked on with interest. Tony was a small-time
dope dealer serving the juvenile market in my
neighborhood. With a 12-year-old at home, I was
more than willing to eliminate Tony from the gene
pool. Tony backed down and apologized.

When I returned from a week's vacation, Tony
had been fired for threatening to beat up a female
supervisor. Quin had a week left to go before he
took another job and seemed to be very worried
about my safety. One night I was discussing an incident with Mike, an older black co-worker. I had
been threatened by three young men on the way to
work. Quin cut in and asked, "Were they white or
black?"

"Black," I answered.

He was obviously relieved. As Mike lamented
the fact that his younger "bruthas" were stupid
enough to pick on the only white guy he knew that
wasn't a racist, Quin was trying to say something
with his eyes but wouldn't pursue the point verbally.
I brushed off the discussion. Quin had nearly died of
alcohol poisoning at age 13 and sometimes went
into extreme emotional fits. You could never tell
what was eating at him.

I later found out that he was torn between his
loyalty to Tony, which was based on something to do
with drug use, and his affection for me, which was
based on the fact that I had given him boxing
lessons and was the only man he knew who had not
abandoned his children.

A week after Quin quit, I took a Saturday night
off. This was highly uncharacteristic behavior: I was
a workaholic. The next morning I picked up the
Sunday paper and discovered that a man, who was
about my age, had been attacked 15 minutes before
I would have been walking to work, a half-mile

down the very road that I took to work. An icy chill
went down my spine as I read on.

Four teenaged members of a wannabe gang
known as the Wasted Youth attacked a 30-year-old
man with knives. He fought the boys off but sustained more than 20 cuts in the process. It sounded
like punks flicking away from the lead. Two of the
four attackers had been apprehended by police.

That night, as I got ready for work, I strapped on
the Othello as I had done religiously for the past
couple of years. As soon as I entered the empty
supermarket, the phone began to ring. When I
answered it Quin said, "Jimmy, are you all right?"

"Yeah, why?"

"Are you carryin' that big blade?"

"Yeah, why?"

"I figured that wasn't you last night. You
would'a killed one of those sorry fuckers, and you'd
be in jail anyhow. Be careful, Jimmy. I'll call ya
back."

Two nights later Quin called back.

"Jimmy, you OK?"

"Yeah, why?"

"That guy that got shanked, that was supposed
to be you. Tony gave those idiots free hits of heroin
and told them that you carried a lot of money, when
and where you walked to work, and that you were a
real big dick. The guy they shanked is my buddy's
older brother, and he really fucked those fuckers up.
The two that got locked up are goin' to do some hard
time —we fuckin' know people, man. The two fuckers that ran got their asses beat yesterday, real good.

"Fuckin' Tony's over here in Hamdon trying to
recruit hitters. Told my buddies over here that you
would be carrying plenty of dough on Saturday,
what ya look like—your funny shoes and raggy
clothes—and that you were a real nigger-lovin',

dick! They asked me what I thought—knew I worked over that way.

"I told 'em that you didn't have shit—that you've got fuckin' kids man!—and that you carried this big fuckin' blade and one of 'em would get stabbed. These guys could take you out, Jimmy. They aren't punks. But they're not takin' the job anyhow because Tony just sold 'em some bad shit. He's headed out of town if he's smart. But he might get somebody on ya, so be careful.

"Jimmy, you *are* kind of a dick, but you got a nice family. I like families. If they get ya, I'll get that fucker myself."

The punch line to this sorry little affair can be found in the last chapter of *The Fighting Edge*.

MICKEY, BRING THE MOP

Incident #29-11
Time of occurrence: night
Duration: 30–40 seconds
Perspective: secondhand account related by an employee of the Big Street Tavern, who interviewed the participants for the author

It was closing time at the Big Street Tavern, and Marty asked the five remaining patrons to leave. This resulted in some disagreement, and Beater, a large notorious bar fighter and the de facto bouncer, became involved in an argument with another large man. The shoving match spilled out into the coatroom as Donny, Ed, and Ed's girl (the three other patrons) also began arguing.

Once all five patrons were in the coatroom, the shoving match between Beater and his antagonist became to a full-blown brawl. By the time Marty made it to the coatroom, the other three were floor fighting, with Ed punching Donny from a mount and his girl kicking Donny in the head.

By the time Marty broke up Beater and the other big man, there was blood everywhere. Marty and Beater then turned their attention to separating Ed and Donny. After the rowdies left, Marty got to work wiping up the blood, which seemed to be a bit much for a bar fight.

Ed never made it home. His girl took him to the hospital when it became obvious that he had been stabbed. He nearly died in the emergency room, having sustained four stab wounds below the ribs, at least one of which had perforated the liver.

Donny was charged, given a trial date, and released on bail.

BRIAN BARRANGER

Incident #53-24
Time of occurrence: night
Duration: 2–3 seconds
Perspective: first-person defender

"I was a senior in high school, so I would have been 18. It was winter, but not cold. The neighborhood was turning predominantly black, causing a lot of hostility. It was about 1:00 A.M. I was walking home from a party, coming up the alley, when I ran into these guys.

"Words were exchanged. I don't remember what was said. We had been drinking Southern Comfort and beer all night. People said I was doing all kinds of stuff. One guy had a razor knife, and he wasn't trying to hide it. He had it cocked for a slash. A knife would be straight in. But he wasn't going to try poking with a razor. I put my hands up to protect my face—fist out. He caught me on the back of the left hand behind the small knuckles, and it cut down around the outside of the wrist. I didn't feel a thing— I wasn't feeling any pain. Why they took off I don't know. I think there was a car coming up the alley.

"I walked home, hit the bed, and crashed. I woke up about four hours later, and there was blood all over the place. I said, 'Holy shit,' and staggered to the bathroom. I had lost a lot of blood but still didn't feel any pain. My watch was on the night stand. I wore it kind of high on the forearm, and the doctor said that's probably what kept me from bleeding before I went to bed. I must of taken it off in my sleep.

"My parents took me to the hospital, and the police were called. The doctor put 28 stitches in. He said that I was lucky—another quarter of an inch difference either way could have meant the difference between life and death.

"The police were very uncooperative. They kept saying that they didn't want to find out later that things were different. They just wrote it off as an accident, because they said they didn't know what really happened. They didn't want to file a report."

SLEEPY

Incident #56-07
Time of occurrence: night
Duration: more than a minute
Perspective: first-person defender

"This was New Year's Eve. I was living in Lansdowne at the time and was in transit from my grandmother's house. I was tired of waiting for the cab in the rain. There was plenty of snow on the ground, but it had turned to rain and was very unpleasant. I started walking to the #11 bus stop, down Monroe Street to Wilkens Avenue and Washington Boulevard.

"There was at least four white guys on my side of Monroe that I could see. But I was highly intoxicated—the brain is telling me to go around, but the alcohol is telling me to go through. I had been drinking Jack Daniels and Budweiser all night. I think [the attack on me] was racially motivated. One of the whiteboys made a racist comment and swung and hit me. By it bein' snowin' I slipped, and I'm fightin' two from the ground. I gets up en tries to run—I'm running toward Pig Town, a predominantly white area. They bank me en I trips and falls.

"Two of 'um I could have easily dealt with. I was 28, 6 foot, 190. They was young, smaller than me.

"I'm on the ground fightin' two. They're tryin' to position me on the ground. It was very important for me to get off the ground. I'm wrastlin' with two as I rise, en one kicks me and I'm shakin' it off when it happened. I was fightin' four guys—I couldn't see but three while I was down. I can't honestly say I saw the weapon.

"I felt it; I knew I been stabbed. By it being' cold, I felt it when it went in. When it come out, that's when I felt the cold and the actual blade itself—which was warm. He must have had it in his pocket. I never saw it.

"I said, 'You bitch. You whore. You had ta stab me!'

"He said, 'Fuck you, nigger. I ain't stabbbed you yet. You're gonna die today, pal.'

"I runs. And I trips en falls. And I knew I was in trouble when they humped on me again—then I saw the stick. . . .

"Getting' shot was scary, but the stabbing was much more so. With getting' shot you're more afraid than hurt. The stabbin' hurt a lot more than the shootin'.

"I runs and I falls again. That's when I knew I

was in a situation where I had to fear for my life. I had called them all kinds of names for stabbing me and knew it was that kind of fight. I grabbed the stick and swung and hit him—the guy with the black leather jacket who had stabbed me. By me being drunk, I can't say I hit him in the face, but I stopped him from aggressin' and attackin' me. They all stopped by me havin' this stick.

"They see I got this stick—holdin' it with the right hand while I'm holdin' my guts in with my left hand. It looked like chitlins, all white. It [the blade] had gone in above the left hip. I'm tryin' to talk my way out, backin' out. They tryin' to surrounds me, en I runs for my life. Once I saw daylight, I just dropped the stick—holdin' my side en runnin'.

"I saw this cabbie—a white guy—stop en make a U-turn. As he pulled up besides me, I grabbed the door—they right on me—and one of 'um hits me while I dove in. He took me straight to University Maryland Hospital. It was New Year's Eve, after midnight. It it weren't for that cabdriver I think that guy would have killed me, and they wouldn't have found the body till morning.

"After the doctors saw my guts pokin' out they did an exploratory surgery, which was more traumatic than the actual stabbing. I stayed in for two days. The cops asked me what happened. When they saw that I was drunk and the area that I had been in at night, the black cop said, 'What the fuck?! You gotta death wish?' They did they job: gave me a report number and victim's assistance number.

"I was grateful to be alive and out of that situation. I learned a very important lesson: wrong place, wrong time, wrong condition, and life is short.

"I have no racial feelings about the experience. I treat people according to how they treat me. You know, people got their ways of dealin' with you.

The Monroe Street section above Pig Town, where Sleepy was attacked. This is the same area in which Raphael was challenged by one of three "whiteboys" who wielded a lock blade (see Chapter 12).

Statistically, the white guy'll stab you. But it a white guy who saved me and was another black guy who shot me."

OBSERVATIONS

The best published information on group attacks with the blade is *Prison's Bloody Iron: Deadly Knife Fighting Tactics Revealed* by Harold J. Jenks and Michael H. Brown (Desert Publications, 1978, still in print as of this writing).

Virtually all the situations discussed in *Prison's Bloody Iron* happen behind bars, and none were complete enough to include in the Violence Index. However, the three-on-one knife attack against Jenks at a nightclub he was managing offers priceless insight into real combat dynamics.

33 BLADE-ARMED GROUPS AGAINST INDIVIDUALS
(PERCENTAGES)

Weapon	%	AVERAGE Number	Blades	Legal	INFLICTED Injury	KO'd	Death
Razor	12	4	1	25	100	-	-
Knife	79	3	1	19	62	31	19
Shank	9	3	1	67	100	100	67

36 BLADE-ARMED INDIVIDUALS AGAINST A GROUP
(PERCENTAGES)

Weapon	GROUP % Deployment	Size	Legal	SUSTAINED Injury	KO'd	Death	INFLICTED Injury	KO'd	Death
Razor	19	3	43	14	-	-	43	-	-
Knife	69	3	40	16	8	4	64	24	8
Shank	6	4	50	50	50	-	100	-	-
Sword	6	7	50	50	-	-	-	-	-

193 INJURY ATTEMPTS
(PERCENTAGES)

Tactic	% Avg.	No. of Injuries	KO's	Deaths
Slash	27	3	12	6
Slice	15	1	17	10
Stab	52	5	51	27
Slash & Stab	4	8	71	29
Slice & Stab	1	4	100	0
Throw	1	0	0	0

NOTE
The number of strikes attempted is not significantly higher than the number of wounds inflicted. Also note that all overhand injury attempts are stabs, usually multiple stabs.

CHAPTER 12

Taking Them with You

Weapon-to-Weapon Blade Encounters

That is the attitude demonstrated by most everyone who has successfully—and decisively—overcome an armed felon: "The punk screwed up." What goes around comes around, and a determined defender is Fate's discount express come-around. Let's take a look at Kenneth in action against the blade. . . .

KENNETH

Kenneth is in his early 50s, works two full-time security jobs, reminds me more of the late Redd Foxx than anyone I have ever met, and comes to work ready to work—the stick, that is.

At the time of our first interview he had been stationed in a drugstore that has a liquor license, which just happens

We thought it was a real gun. That little girl, she was young—cryin'—him with that gun to 'er head. I did think it was a real gun—but when I noticed it wasn't, I said, "Boy, you fucked up."

Management, they was all cryin, "Security, you gonna git us kilt."

But I said, "Nah, he fucked up."

He says, "No, missa; please missa. I'm sorry. I didn't mean it!"

Huh. Wore his young ass out.

I try ta kill him—took him down, worked 'im with the stick: elbows, knees. He don't walk right to dis day—gotta a case pendin' 'gainst "The Company." But they OK—got da best lawyers in a worl'.

Beat 'em down when they threaten you—'spose ta still be workin' 'em when the police gets there.

—Kenneth,
rent-a-cop from hell

179

to be located in the city's most violent section, right off West North Avenue. (Supermarkets don't sell booze in Maryland.) The shoplifters on the West Side are more dangerous than the muggers in the Northeast. The first thing they steal off the rack is the kitchen knife they're going to use against the security guard when they get caught with 50 sticks of deodorant in their underwear.

Kenneth gets paid a 4-percent bonus for every thieving slimebag he hands over to the cops. But the most important morale boost for him is the knowledge that "The Company" has an egghead squad of legal eagles ready to "back my ass up." According to Kenneth, "It a betta deal than 'Nam, but the company will hang your ass out to dry if you get hurt bad or they can't win the case."

His predecessor and the manager had recently been disabled (permanently) by the Spartacus of knife-wielding shoplifters. And he had lately survived two attempts on his life by vengeful shoplifters who came looking for him: one with a bat, the other with a big stick. So Kenneth gave up the double pay for working the North Avenue location and transferred to a location in a decent suburb of northwest Baltimore. . . .

EARNING 4 PERCENT

Incident #45-14
Time of occurrence: day
Duration: 15–20 seconds
Perspective: first-person defender

"This was the Reisterstown Plaza location. The employees love me out there, the customers and police too. I fight and take a ass-whoopin' too. But the whoopin' only last 'til the police get there—then the table turn. See, I might be losin' the battle, but I be winnin' the war. The police is my posse—and they be a comin'. Young hoppers think, 'I'll take this ole man.' And sometime they do—but they get theirs.

"One time this hopper whoop on me. When the police gets him they take him to the back and cuff his ass to a water pipe, and says to me, 'He lay a hand on you? Let him have it!' And there I goes ta work! That the way it is. They miss me out there. I don't fear the enemy. That the wrong attitude to have. So I don't have it. When they took me outta that store, them people cry.

"It was in the cigar aisle when I notice this young hopper stuffin' his pockets with Christmas candy. It was Christmastime, and I were his Santy Claus. I was polite, says, 'Sir, excuse me, but I need to aks you ta leave.'

"He become nasty en call me a 'white nigger.'

"I says, 'Sir, you gots to leave my store and leave my product where you found it. There ain't got ta be no trouble. Jus' leave, please, sir."

"He says, 'Get away from me, you Uncle Tom.'

"I says, 'Please, sir, I don't want no trouble. Jus' put the candy back and leave.'

"He says, 'You nothin' but a asshole slavin' for The Man.'

I says, 'Yes, sir. What eva you say, sir. I were that when I born, and I'll be that when I die. But you gots to go. And I aks you ta leave my candy. Or I'll have ta put you unda arrest.'

"He push me. That when he fuck up. I says, 'You unda arrest,' and he pull out this butcha knife from under his shirt [demonstrates front right-handed cross draw from belt] and hold it out front, like he got me. He sure enough not know how ta use a knife.

"Right then I forgot about God, my wife, right and wrong, and The Company. I become a pure nig-ger! You pull a gun or knife on me, you mean ta kill me. So you pull a gun on me, I a shot nigga. You pull a knife on me, I a cut nigga. Now it your problem.

"I draw [demonstrates right-handed cross-draw deployment of a telescopic steel baton from belt case on left hip, with draw step], look for what at hand, grab a smock off the handle of a stock cart, step back en twirl [demonstrates one-handed wrap of left wrist and hand while raising baton to ready], en say, 'Come on, boy. You want some? Come ged it.'

"En that dummy come at me like this [demonstrates leading inward slash off of a lunge step]. I step back [demonstrates nice draw step]. He come again [repeats lunging slash to belly]. I step back. He come up the middle [lunging upward slash, and I come in over top [downward block with wrapped forearm] and go ta work [demonstrates sticking downstroke between point of skull and left temple].

"I beat that stick into his brain. Let it stick to his head. Don't pull it back till you drive it in. That where the pain come. Don't know why, just does.

"I keep him down [maintains a trap on knife hand] and stick 'im again. That when the hands go up [the knife clattering to the floor] and the blood come. Oh Lord, it look like someone slaughter a hog! So I go to the ribs, en he go down.

"He on 'is ass, hands overhead, and I acomin', goin' ta work [one or two sets of downward forehand-backhand X cuts to the head as knifer tries to cover]. A course he gettin' unda foot, en I got the steel toes on, so I stomp 'im some.

"I made the arrest. Got the summons yesterday. He charged with trespassin', robbery, assault, and attempted murder. I was the arresting officer. He been behind bars all year. Like I said, I were his Santy Claus. Young hoppers don't learn. . . ."

Our "young hopper" here wouldn't have made much sport for a Caesar in the Roman Coliseum. He led with a short-range weapon against a long-range weapon and then compounded his error by fully committing himself with an upward slash against a prepared opponent armed with a secondary trapping weapon.

Of course, I feel so sorry for all of Kenneth's male attackers that I am compelled to offer two examples of weapon use that will make the Christmas candy bandit look like Charles Bronson.

THUMBS DOWN

Incident #51-01
Time of occurrence: day
Duration: 15 minutes!
Perspective: Dan Funk, eyewitness

"I was 13. We lived in Benavon Heights. It was a money part of town, a semirich area. But there was always fights. Our babysitter, Lynn, was 16. One day she said, 'There's going to be a knife fight at the park between Paul and Dave.'

"These guys were her age; pseudo-rich kids who were trying to be that late-blooming hippie burnout without the love. There was a lot of macho in the 70s. Everybody had their reputations to build. These guys weren't real fighters. I had knocked out Dave in a fight when I was 12.

"We went to the store and got candy bars, sodas, and licorice to go down and watch the fight. This was outside in the park, and there were about 40 spectators—friends of both parties in attendance. It was a prearranged fight, planned for about a month in advance. We're all thinking there's no way they're going to stab each other with knives. It was just going to be a dance—a bunch of wannabes. There was even going to be a judge!

"They put on their bandannas and pulled their brown Barlow folding knives with rusty blades and started like *West Side Story*, tossing their knives from hand to hand and dancing around for about 10 minutes—a half-hearted effort. People were cheering and egging them on. We were getting bored and started booing.

"That's when Dave finally stabbed Paul in the right leg. It was purely accidental. Paul screams, like [the fight] is real now, and stabs Dave in the inner portion of the left forearm. There was no skill at all. They really started to go at it: kicking and punching each other.

"There was word that some parents were coming. That's when Nadine went out and broke it up. They limped off and sat side by side on the grass crying. It wasn't exactly the Roman Coliseum, but we had a good time."

BITCH SLAPPING CHICORICAN STYLE

Incident #12-32
Time of occurrence: night
Duration: 20–30 seconds
Perspective: Raphael, first-person defender

"This was at Wilkens Avenue and Smallwood in Pig Town, where Saint Agnes Hospital is, near the Purple Goose Saloon. It was dusk. I was coming from a friend's house with Saib, a Mexican. As we turned left on Smallwood across the street from the Purple Goose, we spotted these three whiteboys in the school yard across the street. One of them said, 'You better stay on that side of the street.'

"I never had this many problems in Chicago. I think Baltimore sucks. A lot of racism here in Baltimore, mostly between blacks and whites. There is no large Hispanic community. You're either white or black. Blacks treat you like you're white. And Caucasians consider us like niggers.

"They were from a little clique that called themselves the Dog House Boyz—you don't have real gangs here in Baltimore. He was mouthing off from across the street. I don't even know why he had a beef with me—probably about some girl in the neighborhood. [Raphael is quite a lady's man.]

Saib was to my left and slightly ahead on the sidewalk as we walked behind these four parked cars. The whiteboys were on the opposite walk as "the mouth" cut diagonally across the street toward me. I didn't see anything. His right hand was down behind his hip. Saib cut between the two parked cars ahead of me and said to the two backup boys, 'You all better stay where you're at.' He said to me, '*El tiene un filete.*' ("He has a knife'.)

"He said to the white kid, 'What you gonna do with that?'

"The whiteboy was about 15 feet ahead when a bell went off in my head. I already had the antennas as a self-defense against the numbers, not against a weapon. See, the antennas are on the passenger side, on the right side of the vehicle.

"People don't realize the weapons that are around you in the street. The car antenna—even if you pop it when it's down—it will still extend once you start spinning it. When you snap it at a rib it will slice you and dice you. If the end breaks, it will work like a razor. The velocity is what gets you. When you use an antenna it gives you the distance. He's got to move in—extend, got to reach—giving me the advantage. That leaves him with the wrong weapon for the wrong range of combat.

"He didn't know I was armed. I had my hands down by my sides as I came around from behind the second parked car. I had the advantage.

"When he pulled the lock blade out to the side I said, 'So you want to play with knives? I'll take that knife and make you into a Popsicle.'

"I don't know why I would say something like that. But, you know, you get frustrated and tired of these people.

"Saib positioned himself to cut off the other two in case they decided to get involved.

"When I saw the blade, I took the antenna to the side and started the sinawali (double-stick pattern). I figured he would have to stick me because he couldn't slice through the sinawali.

"He squared off and started pacing, but couldn't time me, so he came after me with that fencer thing. He was trying to put space between him and myself and was unsuccessful. Every time he stuck it out and tried to fan me with his left, I'd hit him with two X-cuts, so he's getting hit four times.

"He backs up and pulls back the knife, leaving his chest open. I could see that all he had was that brute mentality and street stupidity—no martial skill. My confidence grew the moment he tried to use that fencing—southpaw—lunge. He kept opening up his centerline.

"I moved in with smaller circles. I mean I was whacking the shit out of his hands, because the knife went flying—I don't know where. And then I started bitch-slapping him. He didn't want a fight no more and tried to run between two parked cars. I went after him until he ran behind his boys and kept running. They were laughing at him.

"That was no fight at all. That was an ass whoopin."

FINGER PAINTING ON ROUTE 40

Incident #13-15
Time of occurrence: night
Duration: unknown
Perspective: news report

Two men were reported to be fighting with knives in a motel room on U.S. 40, locally known as

Pulaski Highway, where most of the area motels are located. By the time the police showed up, estimates of which ranged from 5 to 45 minutes, both men were dead. That must have been a great fight! But whom do you interview? Nobody could know just what went down. Here's my best guess.

Whatever weapons used were brought to the scene. Motels don't even provide Sporks, let alone butcher knives. The blades were probably folders, most likely lock blades.

There is no evidence indicating that the over-hand posture has ever been used against an armed opponent. We may assume that it was not used in this case. The lead is almost never used at close quarters. But when two knifers go at it, there is a tendency for the combatants to flow back and forth from ready to lead to ready, although this is more common outdoors. My guess is that one of these guys fought from the lead at some point.

Most fights that occur within the rooms of dwellings involve clinching and floor fighting. Throwing is primarily an outdoor activity. Did the inevitable grab-and-stab stay up against a wall or roll out onto the bed or floor? Considering the obvious intensity of the encounter I'll bet it went to the floor.

Was the action decisive? You bet! One or both of these guys achieved their aim. My guess would be that the aggressor killed his man outright and then bled to death on the spot.

This newspaper story has haunted me for years. Wondering what went down in that cheesy little room was one of the chief motivations behind the study that resulted in this book.

I did this interview on my porch one hot July afternoon and was momentarily horrified when Raphael walked along the sidewalk and grabbed the antenna of my neighbor's new Grand Am. Fortunately, he only extended it, leaving it in place.

FIRST BLOOD, BOY!

Incident #13-03
Time of occurrence: day
Duration: 1 second
Perspective: eyewitness

Larry was a cantankerous World War II veteran, affectionately known as Cigar Face by the boys on his grocery crew. Larry loved challenging the young punks to a tussle so he could put them in an arm lock and make them say uncle.

Larry's sidekick was aptly named Bonehead. Bonehead priced all the products in the cases that Larry cut the tops off and considered this to be an onerous task, yearning to be the cutter and lording it over some lowly pricer, preferably Larry. Not wanting to be made to say uncle, Bonehead opted for a blade challenge. How he figured that a guy who had waited for the kamikazes off of Okinawa would be afraid to cross box-cutter blades with him beats me.

Larry promptly agreed, saying, "First blood, boy!" as he fingered his trusty tool. Bonehead extended his hand to shake on the deal only to have Larry slash open a finger and declare himself victorious. He then cussed out Bonehead for bleeding on his stockroom floor, as he cut open cases at an accelerated rate and threw them across the table, barking one command after another.

Razor use is never heroic, usually tragic, and sometimes comical.

POINTS TO CONSIDER

On those odd occasions when a knifer meets an antagonist armed with a weapon, there are two factors that tend to limit the intensity of the encounter:

- If one party has an obviously inferior weapon, the lesser-armed combatant tends to disappear.
- If both parties are similarly armed, a one-sided fight is the rule. In such cases, the dominant fighter usually holds a monopoly on the attributes crucial for success:
  —Experience
  —Aggressiveness
  —Moral or emotional justification
  —Skill resulting from deliberate preparation

The chances that a man armed with a blade will face another armed with a blade or similar hand weapon in a duel are less than 10 percent, at the moment the knifer deploys his weapon. When one also considers that most blade carriers are not experienced blade users and that fewer than 5 percent of blade users are trained in the use of their weapons, it becomes obvious that a "match fight" with blades is a very rare event. However, it is an event worth preparing for. The rarer the occurrence, the ruder the reality.

I belief that aggressiveness is the key factor. Experience in this area is not something you want, and your skills may not be fully applicable to a given spontaneous situation. But all successful knifers demonstrate extreme aggression.

OTHER POINTS TO CONSIDER

For additional information on blade-to-blade encounters, I recommend Vito Quattrocchi's *The Sicilian Blade: The Art of Sicilian Stiletto Fighting* (Desert Publications, 1993).

Again, none of the real fight accounts in *The Sicilian Blade* were detailed enough to be used in the Violence Index, but the author does offer some real eyewitness insights into knife combat. The last chapter is a must-read for any aspiring knife fighter. The author also makes a good case for using the lead in a blade fight, a case that few knife experts try to make.

For some good old-fashioned American butcher work, read *James Bowie: Texas Fighting Man, A Biography* by Clifford Hopewell (Eakin Press, 1994).

SUMMARY OF WEAPON-TO-WEAPON BLADE ENCOUNTERS

WEAPONS			AGGRESSOR					DEFENDER			
Index	Aggressor	Defender	DR	Med.	Leg.	KO'd	Dth.	Med.	Leg.	KO'd	Dth.
51-01	folder	folder	N	Y	N	N	N	Y	N	N	N
52-01	folder	folder	A	N	N	N	N	N	N	N	N
15-07	fixed	sword	D	N	N	N	N	N	N	N	N
52-21	bat	shank	N	Y	Y	N	N	Y	Y	N	N
51-02	belt	razor	A	N	N	N	N	N	N	Y	N
12-25	razor	folder	D	N	N	N	N	N	N	N	N
13-03	razor	razor	A	N	N	N	N	Y	N	N	N
Note	fixed	fixed	D	Y	N	Y	N	Y	N	N	N
01-13	fold/j	fold	A	N	N	N	N	Y	N	Y	N
13-08	folder	folder	D	N	N	N	N	Y	N	Y	Y
13-15	folder?	folder?	A	Y	N	Y	Y	Y	N	Y	Y
48-08	fold/j	folder	A	N	N	N	N	Y	N	Y	N
45-14	fixed	stick/j	D	N	N	N	N	Y	Y	Y	N
53-21	fold/j	folder	A	N	N	N	N	Y	N	Y	N
52-01	fixed	guns	D	N	N	N	N	N	N	N	N
52-05	guns	fixed	A	Y	N	N	N	Y	N	Y	Y
53-22	bottle	fixed	N	Y	Y	N	N	Y	Y	N	N

NOTES

j = jacket/coat　　　DR = decisive resolution

A = aggressor　　　D = defender

N = no　　　Y = yes

Mike's tale from *True Tales of American Violence* by Chris Pfouts was not part of the Violence Index.

CHAPTER 13

Flesh against Steel

Unarmed Successes against the Blade

*Life has meaning only in
the struggle
Triumph or defeat is in the
hands of the Gods. . . .*

—Swahili war song

My opinion about the best way to defend against the blade is worth about as much as your opinion. And if your opinion was the only thing you needed to base your self-defense study on, you wouldn't have bothered to read this book.

Throughout the book, I have presented various real-life examples of blade or shank use that resulted in a successful defense by an unarmed party. There are many different types and intensities of possible blade encounters. Unfortunately, most victims of the blade attacks I have documented do not even attempt a coherent defense, let alone succeed. This makes unarmed successes against the blade rare and most certainly worthy of study.

In this chapter I will present successful actions—not defenses—against a blade or shank by an unarmed party. A successful action is defined as a decisive resolution in favor of the unarmed party. Whether or not one defines success or failure based on injuries sustained reflects personal values and cannot be defined objectively. A facial scar would be a badge of honor for Russel; an interesting talking point for Duncan; a résumé enhancement for Raphael; a personal disaster for Faith, a beautiful socialite who survived a mugging; and a financial disaster for the New York fashion model who had her face slashed with a razor back in the 1980s.

In my mind victory and defeat are subjective. If I step into the boxing ring against the heavyweight champion of the world and get KO'd in the first round, that's a win for me as long as I'm alive to collect my check. You might think I'm nuts, but imagine yourself, man or woman, in the following situation:

You are 85 and dying of brain cancer. As you step outside you see three teenaged thugs dragging your beautiful granddaughter behind the bushes in the backyard. If you call the police and finish watching your soap opera until the cops show up and then go out back and identify the body, you have avoided injury (the stated objective of most self-defense systems). But you have failed on a practical, spiritual, and genetic level.

If, on the other hand, you hobble around back and attack the rapists with your frying pan until you die of a massive coronary or they stomp you into geriatric pudding, you will have given your granddaughter a chance to escape and, at the very least, given the rapists a reason to flee the scene rather than continue their attack on the apple of your eye. Now, that sounds like a win to me. Of course, it's not a win to your granddaughter.

The "victory" is not what I'm trying to qualify when I study violence. I define a decisive resolution as having imposed one's will on the adversary. If both parties are suicidal and both define victory as killing the other party no matter their own fate, then they are both winners if they tumble off a cliff together. If your intent was to make your adversary say uncle and he did, you have attained a decisive resolution—even if you are ultimately "the loser" because he was HIV positive and commingled his blood with yours before he submitted.

"I'M HAIRIER THAN YOU ARE!"

Incident #41-17
Time of occurrence: night
Duration: seconds
Perspective: Duncan, first-person defender

"This was right before I went into the navy. I was still a skinny kid. I was up at Riverside Park arguing with my ex-girlfriend when this bigger, older guy comes down the hill showing this blade. He was trying to be her knight in shining armor— you know, trying to get some. I forget exactly what I said, but I did tell him that if he put the knife away I wouldn't kill him with it. He left. Perhaps he knew about me from the neighborhood.

"I'm not afraid of knives. I've been cut on the job. Unless there's meat hanging out, I just tape the cuts up with duct tape. A person who pulls a knife on me is letting me know that they need it. Pussies use knives."

YO MONAY'S MA MONAY

Incident #21-02
Time of occurrence: day
Duration: 3–4 seconds
Perspective: first-person defender

Vernon was working behind his bread truck in the parking lot of a supermarket in Spanish Harlem when an average-looking young man approached him with a lock blade in his lead right hand and said, "I wan' yo monay."

Vernon responded, "And?"

"I say, 'I wan' yo monay!'"

"And?"

The knifer made a leading inward cut (the surest sign of incompetence with the blade). Vernon avoided this with a single sliding step back and to his right, away from the blade.

The knifer said, "Oh, I see. I'll get you mutha-fuca," and made a second inward cut, with the same result. But he then seemed to become afraid, looked around, and ran off.

Vernon, though he is not a martial artist, used his basic athletic ability to maintain his personal space and keep the knifer from bridging the distance. Certain kung-fu teachers regard the execution of this concept as a high skill indicative of martial arts mastery. The more functional Chinese fighting arts place a high premium on such basics as maintaining distance and staying on your feet. If you peel away the useless embroidery that enshrouds these systems, you will find some applicable skills useful against the blade, in contrast to the suicidal blade defenses of many Asian arts.

ACCIDENTAL PERFECTION

Incident #12-28
Time of occurrence: day
Duration: 5 seconds
Perspective: first-person defender

This common blade-armed robbery posture is usually directed at boys and old men. The attacker often has a flanking accomplice. Female victims are usually grabbed and warned. If perceived as dangerous, male targets are often cut or stabbed outright. (Photo by Khristopher Kramer.)

Two punks I was working with decided to threaten me with their butterfly knives. The fact that their unarmed intimidation tactics had been ineffective was bothering them. I could tell that the fat one was going to draw, and I could have cut him easily, but I wanted to keep my job. I believed his intention was to hold the blade to my belly and intimidate me—as a warning.

These weren't active criminals but wannabes. Without a moment's thought I acted instinctively, and it worked! I never practiced or envisioned the following sequence.

The fat guy attempted a lead right-hand draw from a nylon Velcro case worn laterally (flap to groin) on his belt between his right hip and buckle. I was directly to his front. His partner stood momentarily frozen to his right.

I stepped on his right foot with my left as I trapped his right hand with my open left, which I had held against my own hip. We were hip to hip. He stepped back to gain space for his draw. I shifted my weight onto his foot, and let my right foot slide as he slid back. He outweighed me by 90 pounds but was so focused on the blade that he just dragged me with him.

As he tried to muscle his hand out from under mine and step back simultaneously, I shifted my weight forward again and pressed my right fist against his lips. He raised his left hand in a gesture of surrender and said, "Okay."

I stepped off his foot and placed my right hand on the butt of the utility knife that was sheathed between the buckle of my leather work belt and the button of my blue jeans.

"You guys wanna go with blades?"

They didn't offer a coherent reply.

I said, "You guys probably draw them things 50

times a day. I freight 300 pieces a night with his thing. Who do ya think's gonna get cut first?"

I emphasized the point by drawing (without sliding) the blade forward and dragging the blade slot of the utility knife across his chest with a backhand and back across his throat with a forward stroke with a right-hand step. This placed me to his extreme right, with his body between me and his knife hand and his friend. There was no need to elaborate.

The next time I was scheduled to work with these two, the sidekick showed up first. I motioned for him to follow me into the frozen food storage unit (a commercial walk-in), and he followed. I drew the Othello from behind my left hip and executed a rapier thrust, driving the blade to the hilt through a case of frozen fries, pulling the blade out with the aid of my boot heel. He chuckled, swallowed hard, and walked away.

An hour later his mentor brought me a well-used butterfly knife. He no longer wore the belt case. As he handed the blade over he said, "I don't think this will ever do me any good. You can have it."

I explained that the knife wasn't really practical for big men and that he'd be better off throwing me against a wall.

The blade threat attempted by the young punk in that warehouse barely qualifies as violence; even by my standards it is a 1 on the 1-to-10 scale. It could have been much worse. At his age, I would have cut his throat in the same situation, resulting in prison time. At 25 I would have broken his nose and taken the knife as a trophy, resulting in my loss of employment. But experiencing some tense situations and training to relax in the ring and on the mat gave me the poise and skills to make it a nonevent.

The dynamic duo ceased wearing their stylish blades and soon became firearm enthusiasts. They did, however, do me one final service. . . .

Greg was a truck driver who shared our equipment on the dock and in the warehouse. We only knew one another through passing glances and nods of respect as we went about our business. One fine day the duo was threatening Greg with bodily harm if he used the tow motor—this to a guy who could have been a pro wrestler or middle linebacker. I was struck dumb by this insane behavior until I realized how diabolical my punk co-workers were.

Greg said, "All right, you two think you can take me?"

They said in unison, "No, but he can," pointing their milquetoast fingers at me. "He's a bad dude. He'll beat your ass. In fact," said fat boy, "we'll put up 20 bucks apiece that says you can't take him."

At this point Greg and I were eyeing each other with interest. I was beginning to respect these guys. They were going to get me yet. We were standing, with the punks to my right and his left, on an 8x12-patch of treated concrete surrounded by stacks of wooden pallets, cardboard bales, and steel carts loaded with canned goods. These creeps had put us in a position where one of us had to back down. If not, for $20 apiece, they would get to see two of their detested oppressors maim one another.

Greg was a muscular 6 feet, 4 inches, 250 pounds, with good looks and hard lines accented by his military-style haircut. He had the most to lose by backing down and the least to lose in a fight. I noticed with dread that he first looked at the floor, a fighting surface that would favor me. He took it for granted that I was what they had said. He then body-typed me from feet to shoulders (big guys only bother to body-type small men if they have fought tough small men in the past). He then looked behind me and to the sides to measure the space available. After his eye caught the stack of pallets to my back he looked at the button flaps of my open flannel shirt and then—most ominously—to my long hair. He then clenched his jaw, looked me in the eyes without malice or kindness, and said, "Well? What do you say?"

My turn. He was twice my mass, with at least four times my strength, and he knew that he had to grab me—which meant that he had at least as much experience as I. He was athletic enough to catch me if he was willing to get hit a lot. The fact that he clenched his teeth told me he knew all about eating punches. I had sparred fearless heavyweights at close quarters and knew I had 10 to 20 seconds before the inevitable clinch with a wall of muscle. If I beat the 30-second margin I'd probably break my hands. I had to find a way out.

Remembering who my enemies were, I pointed to the two twerps and said, "I'll bet you 50, straight up, that I can KO the fat one before you can catch the skinny one."

He grinned and said, "Deal!"

By the time we turned they were gone.

I walked up to Greg and said, "That would have been fun, " as we shook hands.

He said, "What about us?"

"That wouldn't have been fun."

"How do you think it would have gone?"

"I would have made you look really stupid for about 15 seconds. Then you would have made me look really ugly until you got sick of the mess."

"Yeah, that's about what I figured. I'm not much of a boxer. Mostly I use the ground."

We had a long talk afterward, during the course of which I discovered that I had avoided a brawl with a former champion bar fighter, who once served as a sparring partner for his older brother, an amateur boxer.

As for the dynamic duo, they soon retired from punk life and have since become respectable citizens.

TATTOO RICK

Incident #48-13
Time of occurrence: night
Duration: seconds
Perspective: first-person aggressor

Tattoo Rick was tending bar at his place on U.S. 1 when Crazy Billy, an unloved patron, pulled out his butterfly knife and began twirling it around.

"I specifically remember him sticking it into the top of the barrel there [points to a barrel used as a beer stand]. By the time he pulled it out and started waving it around again, I had come around from behind the bar and was behind him. He was holding the thing straight out in front of him with his right hand, pointed at nobody in particular.

"I stepped out to his right side and slapped down on his biceps [demonstrates with left hand] while I slapped up on his forearm [demonstrates with right]. The knife ejected over his shoulder, and I followed through with a throw [demonstrates sweeping heel throw on hapless author], which definitely fucked his night up. He was out. I collected his knife, put it in his knit cap, stuffed it under his sweatshirt, and dragged him across to the car wash.

"Dragging these fuckers 50 feet from the bar door is the toughest part of the job. Fortunately, this guy was little, like you. This is why I prefer to talk the bigger idiots as far out the door as possible before kicking their asses. No sense in hauling all that if you don't have to."

If you ever want a stern pro-union lecture, stop into the Cafe Tattoo and order an ice-cold Coors Light.

BEWARE THE BIG JOHNSON

Incident #22-13
Time of occurrence: night
Duration: less than a minute
Perspective: Crazy Steve Newman, first-person defender

"We're drinking down the Garden. It's late; about 12:30. The ex-old lady and her friend are there, and we're talking about sex. When this boy—a big boy, bigger than me—comes up to me talking shit and reaches in his pants. I say, 'Boy, get the fuck away from me,' and he starts whipping it out. So bam! [demonstrates stepping head-butt, nearly KOing author] I rocked his world, Jimmy! Right in the face.

"And this fucker tries whipping it out again, so I grab his nuts like this [I'm thankful he demonstrates by grabbing his own crotch], and bam! [demonstrates head-butt, pushing the author's bandanna down over his eyes]. And this boy backs up and tries to whip it out again. So I says. 'Boy, yer fuckin' with me!' And wham! [demonstrates shoulder-shove/heel-throw on imaginary opponent]. And I'm hot for this motherfucker! 'Come on, boy.' I'm ready ta fuck his world up right there—and my buddies break it up and take him outside.

"I'm like, 'Yeah, motherfucker. Boy, you and me outside.'

"When my buddies come back, they say this boy's got a fucking serrated butcher knife in his pants! They told me not to go after him. 'Fuck!' I thought, 'he was trying to show his dick off.' I didn't expect a knife—one with teeth! When I left he was gone. He was a big boy too. That's a mean boy ta pull a knife on a smaller guy."

PRIMAL RESPONSE

Incident #27-04
Time of occurrence: night
Duration: about a minute
Perspective: Dan Funk, first-person defender

"We were in a college bar in North Hills (Pittsburgh). There was a fairly large group of us wrestlers who drank and roamed around together. We were pretty rowdy with one another—within the group—but generally started no trouble with others. Perhaps half were also football players. If there's any trouble with wrestlers' starting fights it would be these types: the football players. The pure wrestlers tend to be less aggressive drinkers and hold up much higher academic standards. On the college level, wrestlers are your most accomplished scholar-athletes.

"It was autumn. We had been having a good time amongst ourselves when this guy began looking across the bar at me. Later he approached and started talking shit. Why he selected me I don't know. He was 6 foot, 165. I'm wrestling 190 at the time. He says, 'You think you're tough. You guys come in here like you own the place.'

"He continues in an egotistical vein—weight-lifter, boxer, martial artist, etc. I proceeded to ignore him, and this cat went back, sat down, and glared. He was seated with friends. However, the more he drank the more quiet he became. His friends began to drift away.

"He approached me again as I stood at the bar, and it felt like I got punched in the solar plexus. I just dropped down, grabbed him by the legs, picked him up, took him over my right side, and slammed him down. I took him right because I wanted to lead with his head when I planted him. There was no ancillary fighting going on. But in a bar situation you don't want to get under somebody because you don't know who they're with. You might have two or three guys laying boots into you.

"As a wrestler in a fight, you don't want to go to the ground unless you're going to be the one on top. You don't shoot! You level-change—change your level relative to the opponent. The guy might have one year of high school wrestling and be able to sprawl your shoot, and then you've got a big guy pounding on you.

"I took him over my side, and we came down hard. He just grunted out. At that point I didn't even see anything in his hand. He was out.

We left within a minute. The deal with a bar fight is you get out in a hurry, not only to avoid the police, but because people come back, and a lot of times things will go down.

"I started feeling warmth in my chest area. I noticed a patch of blood on my shirt. I pulled up my shirt and there was a pattern of about five holes over my solar plexus—pretty much dead center. He had stabbed me with a broken bottle. The doctors were worried because of the location and kept me for a while. It healed up pretty well, though it did scar.

"I never saw, or heard, or felt, the bottle."

(Dan Funk is still wrestling in shoots at age 34.)

SUMMARY OF SUCCESSFUL UNARMED
DEFENSES AGAINST THE BLADE

Index	Weapon	Defense	KNIFER				DEFENDER			
			Med.	Leg.	KO'd	Dth.	Med.	Leg.	KO'd	Dth.
12-28	knife	trap	N	N	N	N	N	N	N	N
12-32	knife	kick/hold	N	N	Y	N	N	N	N	N
12-35	razor	throw	N	N	N	N	N	N	N	N
13-10	knives	punch/throw	N	Y	N	N	Y	N	N	N
19-12	razor	hold	N	Y	N	N	Y	N	N	N
22-03	knife	butt/gouge/th	N	N	N	N	N	N	N	N
27-04	shank	throw	Y	N	Y	N	Y	N	N	N
36-16	sword	hold	N	Y	N	N	N	N	N	N
41-04	knife	throw	Y	N	N	N	Y	N	N	N
41-06	shank	hold/punch/throw	Y	N	Y	N	Y	N	N	N
41-17	knife	verbal	N	N	N	N	N	N	N	N
42-15	knife	hold	N	Y	N	N	Y	N	N	N
46-16	knife	hold	Y	N	N	N	N	N	N	N
47-09	knife	kick	N	N	N	N	N	N	N	N
49-20	shank	hold	Y	Y	N	N	Y	N	N	N
52-16	knife	punch	N	Y	N	N	Y	N	N	N
53-17	knife	hold	N	N	N	N	Y	N	N	N

NOTES
Y = yes;   N = no

23 SUCCESSFUL UNARMED TACTICS (PERCENTS)

Hold	35
Throw	26
Punch	13
Kick	9
Trap	4
Butt	4
Gouge	4
Verbal	4

RECOMMENDED READING

If you would like to define your own knife defense doctrine I recommend the following material:

1. Diaz-Cobo, Oscar. *Unarmed against the Knife*. Boulder, Colo.: Paladin, 1982 (out of print). Oscar makes a strong case for striking against the knifer.
2. Pentecost, Don. *Put 'em Down, Take 'em Out!: Knife Fighting Techniques from Folsom Prison*. Boulder, Colo.: Paladin, 1988. Don shows you how to kill an unarmed man using a shank. This is a priceless perspective.
3. Quinn, Peyton. *Defending against the Blade* (video). Boulder, Colo.: Curve Productions, 1990. Peyton makes a strong case for grappling and handguns.

CHAPTER 14

Living to Fight Another Day

All about Running Away

People are more afraid of knives than guns because they know what knives do. You don't pull out a gun and shoot your steak at the dinner table.

—Duncan

When asked what to do when confronted with an edged weapon, many self-defense instructors tell their students to run away or leave the scene. Although this advice makes more sense than the alternative defenses—usually consisting of wrist manipulation fantasies—it leaves much to be desired.

Advising Tuck, 50 years of age and 350 pounds, to run from the next twerp who pulls a knife on him makes as much sense as telling Pepper, 40 years old and 100 pounds, to punch out the next heavyweight prizefighter who decides to rape her.

Running away is as dynamic, subjective, and unique to the situation at hand as is the spontaneous combat it is meant to avoid. This is a subject that I have very little firsthand knowledge of. You see, for me running is not an option. My number-one priority as a father is to maintain my employment. I make my living lifting things. As can be expected, this has resulted in both chronic and catastrophic injuries to the lower back. The worst thing a mugger can do to me is put me out of work and on my back.

By far, the worst beatings I have taken were dished out in gym fights at the hands of my own boxing pupils. When they can make the old man look like a car wreck survivor, they've graduated. The last two bloody graduation showers I threw for my boys resulted in dozens of visible raised bruises, along with swallowing a half-pint of my own precious fluids.

The beating that the heavyweight gave me was so well executed that more than one felonious co-worker of mine asked if they could hire him for some "work." The starching I took from the lightweight wasn't as disfiguring, but did result in some structural damage. The next day, when I entered my doctor's office to have my chest carti-lage decompressed so I could regain full use of my left lung, his receptionist broke into tears. When Doctor Wayne entered the exam-ination room he said over his shoulder, "No, he wasn't in an auto accident. He just fought the wrong guy."

The point is that neither of these beatings resulted in loss of work time. However, the last time I chased a soccer ball I lost thousands of dollars in income and spent many long days flat on my back. The last time I ran (actually jogged) a block for a bus, I missed a week of work. I'm fighting. Better ugly than crippled.

Even this doesn't touch on the main point one should consider when deciding whether or not to run: Can I get away? If so, how? This is where experience in ball sports and the ability to body-type strangers correctly is crucial.

To explore the ins and outs of hide preservation through inglori-ous evacuation, I have consulted various witnesses and participants of real-life chases. Since blade encounters rarely present the defend-er with a reasonable opportunity to run, most of the information available on flight is general and has to be extrapolated to cover run-ning from the knifer.

GUMBY

Incident #54-17
Time of occurrence: day
Duration: 15–30 seconds
Perspective: eyewitness

Gumby and Ricky, two 18-year-old boys, were arguing over a girl on the street. Gumby was a chubby stoner with "Fuck You" tattooed on his neck, a White Power tattoo on his shoulder, a goatee, and acid burns on his left side from hand to temple. Ricky was taller, athletic, and "known to beat people up."

Gumby produced a very large screwdriver, grasped in the ice-pick grip, and attempted to stab Ricky. Ricky ran around a parked car away from Gumby's weapon hand and bolted up an alley to his house, with Gumby in pursuit.

Ricky emerged from his house with a baseball bat and went after Gumby, who ran like hell and was not seen for some time.

In his attack on Ricky, Gumby (not yet a mature thug) failed to get close enough to strike before the weapon was seen. Furthermore, the pursuer holds some crucial advantages in any chase. But Ricky had four things going for him: athletic ability, an obstacle (the car), a rising grade to run up (the alley), and an object for aggressive use in his baseball bat.

WALKING THE DOG

Incident #12-27
Time of occurrence: day
Duration: 1 second
Perspective: Sammy, first person

"I thought he was a jogger. But he stabbed me right here [left forearm] as he ran past [from behind]. He kept goin! Was just walkin' my dog in the park. Didn't recognize the guy."

TOO QUICK

Incident #41-05
Time of occurrence: day
Duration: 10–20 seconds
Perspective: first-person aggressor

Mike was helping Ed, a licensed bounty hunter. A bail jumper was hiding in his own mother's house. To flush him out, Ed took the front, Mike, the back. The jumper emerged from the basement stairwell and was off like a shot down the alley.

Mike and Ed converged behind the jumper as he emerged from the alley onto a sidewalk. He was losing them easily, ducking and darting like a running back between pedestrians. As he broke into a dead run, he looked over his shoulder and ran straight into a metal light pole. The collision sounded like the tolling of a giant bell and knocked the jumper out cold.

SMACKDADDY JAY

Incident #54-20
Time of occurrence: night
Duration: seconds
Perspective: Puppet, first-person aggressor

"SmackDaddy was a part-time pimp, clerking with me on the East Side, and 'runnin' a string a ho's' on the West Side. While heading for the bus stop, he was approached by two 'young bruthas' asking for a light. When he reached into his shirt pocket they began punching him. He 'threw back,' knocking out teeth and tearing up his knuckles, and turned and ran, catching the bus."

A HELPING HAND

Incident #47-03
Time of occurrence: day
Duration: 10–15 seconds
Perspective: Kenneth, first-person aggressor

"Today I got one at the day job. This man—he not a young hopper, maybe 35—had a backpack on. He fill it with videotapes en think he gonna outrun me. I old, but not that old. He hoppin' downe da aisle, and I a'comin!

"He sure 'nough not fast. But he did get out the front door. A course he have help. I right behind him, and he go through it open. You know, I pattin' him on the back. A terrible noise. Glass en blood everywhere. He a sittin' in it cryin'. I there. I got the arrest. But I not cuff 'im. Naw, not in that mess. I work 'im instead.

"I don't play, so stealin' form The Company don't pay. Naw, it sure 'nough not pay.'"

SHIN SPLINTS

Incident #15-29
Time of occurrence: night
Duration: seconds
Perspective: Spin, first-person defender

"Yo, ma brutha. Thought Yo a dead nigga! Boy, that was one krazee night!

"Yo, Yo nigga be up-curb, yo evil nigga be serious strapped and lookin' ta nine, and yo smart nigga be down-curb en runnin' down the alley! Thought for sho' he cap Yo ass—but Yo' nigga be pumpin' *down the street!*"

PUPPET

Incident #08-04
Time of occurrence: night
Duration: seconds
Perspective: first-person aggressor

"My second husband, I hid in his mother's house. I was nine months pregnant and due any day. I thought he was going to kill me. I went to the bar and found him after he had been out for three days, ordered a beer, and sat down between him and his friend.

"They were joking around and carrying on. Then they started talking about women they had met at another bar. I went to the bathroom and started crying; then I came out—I didn't have any of this planned—and I grabbed him by his hair and shook him back and forth, trying to kill him—hoping I would break his fucking neck.

"I was really mad—had been home by myself. He was holding on to the bar. Then I flung him, and the molding broke off the bar while he flew to the floor. All his friends were laughing at him.

"I hid in his mother's house. But he didn't come, so I snuck back into the bar—he was still there—and had the barmaid give me his change. He said if I ever did that again he would kill me. I really thought he would. I said, 'Fuck you.'

"That was it. We drank a couple more beers and went home."

This incident illustrates the same point that hit-and-run muggers make all the time: the best time to run is just after you have struck a blow and set the other party back on his heels or, better yet, on the floor.

THE ROAD RUNNER

Incident #54-18
Time of occurrence: day
Duration: less than a minute
Perspective: Bryant, first-person aggressor

The Road Runner was a famous shoplifter known throughout South Baltimore for his ability to outrun even the fleetest retail clerk. The clerks at the thrift store on Light Street had given up on the Road Runner, until Bryant, a lanky young kickboxer, said, "Somebody's gotta catch 'im."

The chase covered two city blocks and involved dodging and hurdling parked and moving vehicles. "The Road Runner was a short, fast sombitch, but I side-hurdled a parked car and clipped him into the wall of the Cross Street Market—broke his stride. He took a swing, which I slipped, and flew into the market. That's where I caught 'im. He punched me two or three times and I slammed his head down into the glass display case and held him. He was done.

"I've takin' down many a shoplifter. Generally the longer they run, the better—wear 'em out. The longer they run, the longer they got that fear in 'em. It drains 'em. Pushing them is the easiest way to break their stride—that's all you have to do—break their stride. Clip 'em, tackle 'em, grab 'em, push 'em—it all works."

What Bryant is pointing out is the loss of stamina and erosion of fighting ability resulting from the emotional state of mind of the fleeing party. If the runner is caught, his attacker is very likely behind him and is in an aggressive state, while the runner is still caught in a flight mind-set.

SHOULD YOU RUN?

The opportunity to flee before being cut or stabbed is rarely an option in the case of a serious attack. About half of cutting and stabbing targets do have a reasonable chance of running after the attack begins. If the attacker really knows what he's doing, you are going to be in a fight.

If the knifer leads with the weapon, he is indicating a reluctance to attack, and attacking includes pursuit. If he shows the blade deliberately, you can probably walk without triggering a pursuit, especially if you are not cornered.

However, there are the incompetent maniacs like Gumby out there who mean to kill you but show their hand too early, giving you a chance to ponder an escape.

Trust your instincts on this one. If you are more confident in your ability fight than in your ability to outrun an attacker, do not give him your back. Fight him. If you decide otherwise, you need to assess his pursuit options as well as your flight options. Such factors are unique to the situation.

COMMON PURSUIT FACTORS

The following are factors common to most chase situations.

- The pursuer is more focused than the pursued. He has a specific objective: you!
- The pursuer has the option to dive for a tackle. The pursued does not have a similar option.

SPECIFIC PURSUIT FACTORS

The following factors, unique to each situation, determine whether you should run or not.

- Knifers using the ice-pick grip have consistently demonstrated a willingness and ability to pursue and have been the only ones to succeed in stabbing on the run. Assume that a knifer in this posture will pursue. If he switches to this grip as you make a move to leave, know that he will pursue.

- A knifer using a natural grip is in jeopardy of falling on his own blade if he trips, will have a hard time tackling without losing the blade, will not be able to strike effectively against a target moving away from him, and will break his stride if he does attempt a strike on the run.
- A person running with something gripped in his hand—whether a baton, football, baseball glove, or knife—will not attain the same foot speed as he would if he were empty-handed.
- Groups are more likely to pursue their victims than are individuals—and more likely to catch their prey. Multiple pursuers can fan out and limit your dodging options.
- Foot speed at short distances—sprinting—is very much a function of strength and aggressiveness. Like a grizzly bear, many big men are deceptively quick in the sprint.

HOW AND WHERE TO RUN

- Never ever run down a staircase, hill, or steep grade of any kind. Always run up.
- The best way to initiate a run is to shove your adversary and use his body to push off for your sprint as he is rolling back on his heels. This gives you a double-step lead.
- When you are being pursued by a knifer using an ice-pick grip, dodge away from his weapon-hand side, ideally around an obstacle.
- When you are running from the ready grip, dodge to your opponent's weapon-hand side to avoid being grabbed or pushed with the empty hand.
- Run toward people. They make good speed bumps.
- Run toward the nearest hospital, especially if you have been cut.
- Focus on an ultimate destination. Don't just run around.
- Don't play "George of the Jungle" with light poles.
- Get up a flight of stairs so that you can kick him. Hold on to the railing. Remember that your feet are better protected by your everyday attire than any other portion of your body.

- Remember that your opponent can't grab with the knife hand, so consider clearing obstacles, such as fences, that require gripping.
- Striking from the lead on the run is the knifer's last-gasp effort. The blade will achieve poor penetration if the stroke scores. A missed stroke, which is likely, will ruin the knifer's stride and probably end the pursuit.

WHO TO RUN FROM

A lot of trained fighters are easier to deal with than someone like Duncan. But when it comes to a knife-armed assailant, you can't afford to play around. If you know, suspect, or can decipher from his body mechanics that the guy coming after you with a knife has any striking, grappling, or blade training, I recommend flight *if there is a reasonable chance of success*. And, by all means, if the guy is a former football player and known cokehead, and you happen to be spending time with his old lady, I would definitely avoid testing your soft, warm flesh against his sharp, cold steel.

Early one morning, in the loft of a neighborhood bar, I was losing the third in a series of pool games to Montique, a middle-aged man who happened to be an amateur billiards champion. As I sighted in on the cueball along my cue, he accused me of being a pool shark and trying to lure him into a disastrous wager. Montique claimed, "No martial artist could be that bad at pool. And you are obviously a martial artist. What is your art?"

"Boxing, Western boxing."

A look of utter disgust clouded his face at the mention of boxing as a martial art. It was the kind of look you could expect from the chef of a five-star restaurant as you applied ketchup from the crusted nozzle of a squeeze bottle onto the filet mignon he had cooked.

All of a sudden I suspected I was in the presence of a traditional karate stylist. When he broke into a cat stance to test my reflexes, I knew he was a karate guy. When he tried to get an angle for a front thrust kick I suspected shorin-ryu (and later found this to be the case) and shuffle-stepped out of range. When he came up with the lunge-punch, I took a draw step to his right, which placed the corner pocket between him and me.

He reluctantly nodded his approval, satisfied that he had pegged me as a trained fighter, though still wincing from the bitter taste of a Western art. He quizzed me on vital points, striking surfaces, and the type of stick I trained with. Having decided to allow me to share the title of martial artist, despite my abominable stylistic preference, he nodded for me to take the shot. I scratched, and he ran the table.

A good eye for sound body mechanics, eye-hand coordination, and gait patterns will also help you pick a good runner out of a crowd.

If you are new to combat sports or athletics in general, watch a football game. If your antagonist is built like, or walks like, the guys who start each play on the line of scrimmage, running away is probably your best bet. If, however, your man reminds you more of the guys roaming the offensive and defensive backfield, running away will be the functional equivalent of turning your back to him and grabbing your ankles.

HIDING

As Puppet pointed out to me one overcast morning, hiding is only effective when you hide where your pursuer is not going to look. Having made your initial escape, you must alter whatever fixed patterns you follow—like hanging out at a certain bar—or else you may be caught on your rear, with no place to run, or worse. . . .

BANNO, ON THE CASE

Incident #54-19
Time of occurrence: night
Duration: minutes
Perspective: first-person aggressor

When Banno returned from 'Nam, he maintained his association with an Asian organized crime figure known as "the Prince." Banno was occasionally called on to provide muscle for the Prince's State-side operation. When a small-time operator crossed the Prince and fled "The District," Banno and Jack (a shadowy figure) were called into service.

The ultimate aim of the interstate hunt was not made clear to the author. It did appear to have involved the return of something to The Prince: either goods, cash, or the operator (or a piece of him). Banno and Jack went directly to the locale their prey was known to frequent and caught him in bed with a prostitute.

They had one nickel-plated .44 between them. Banno broke down the door and grabbed their man as he was pulling up his underwear. With Jack covering with the gun, Banno gave the operator a vicious wedgie, tearing the crotch out of his briefs and winding the elastic like a noose around his throat.

Jack wanted to know what the penalty should be for this black man sleeping with a white woman. That's when a dark light went off in Banno's head.

"Put the barrel in his mouth."

"Now what?"

Banno grabbed the terrorized man's belt and bound his wrists behind his back, and then said, "Help me tie the piece to his face."

With their prey sucking on the barrel of Banno's second-favorite pistol, the two men managed to secure the weapon to the operator's face with his own underwear. These "bounty hunters" had parked their car 2 miles away on a rural route; their hideout was at the end of a "red-dog" (broken brick) road, which is murder to walk on.

The man was made to walk naked and barefoot down this road in the dark of night, with his hands bound behind him and a cocked .44 Magnum strapped to his face, as Banno and Jack kicked at his heels and jeered, "Don't trip! We wouldn't want you falling on your face."

At this point in my discussion with Banno—which he did not know was an interview—he became distracted by a naked female cartoon character on his television set crawling through a log. This was an animated flick about a primitive warrior planet, which he regarded as "a classic." He expressed no more interest in our discussion of The Prince.

This story points out the most important aspect of maintaining your margin of safety once you have *temporarily* evaded a pursuer. Running away, even if successful, is only a temporary solution if your pursuer is willing and able to stalk, search for, and *hunt* you.

After the trauma of a chase, your insinct will be to return to a comfort zone (e.g., your apartment). But remember that the more comfortable you would normally feel in your chosen place of rest, the more easily you will be found.

If you ever find yourself caught up in such a situation, think of that figitive drug dealer from the East Coast being walked down that western road by Banno and Jake.

REFLECTIONS ON THE BLADE

Your chances of avoiding a knife attack are very good if you recognize the knifer's approach posture and deny him the preconditions he needs to build the confidence to launch a successful attack. These preconditions are as follows:

- You are unaware of his presence or intent.
- You permit yourself to be isolated or cornered.
- You do not have a potential weapon in your hand.
- The knifer judges you to be incapable of beating him in an unarmed fight (applies primarily to rapes and murders).

As for using a blade for defense, you must remember that if the weapon is too light to use as a club or it is not edged or pointed, the weapon will have little shock value. Also, there is no ultimate grip or stance. Each of the three postures I have identified and studied is appropriate for certain situations and inappropriate for others.

Above all, remember the four keys to victory:

- Experience
- Aggression
- Athletic ability
- Training

These keys apply to all types of combat, and one and two are the big dogs of violence. Don't underestimate the guy who possesses either of these advantages at the outset of an encounter.

In regard to blade fighting, the steel (whether it's yours or his) is a mirror offering the fighter the clearest possible reflection of his own character.

ON BUTCHERS HILL

Incident #13-07
Time of occurrence: day
Duration: 20–30 seconds
Perspective: first-person aggressor

Gary had just turned 18 and was enjoying his new drinking privileges at a bar in the Butchers Hill section of East Baltimore. This section is a few blocks from Patterson Park, where dog handlers train their pit bulls on abducted pets and where I have trained a number of young fighters.

As Gary was enjoying his beer, a Lumbee Indian pulled another Lumbee off a barstool, maintained a hold on his shirt, and stabbed him with five or six ice-pick strokes to the shoulders. The stabbing victim made it to his feet and ran out of his shirt, with the knifer following him to the doorway while stabbing him three more times from the overhand position.

The knifer caught him on the sidewalk in front of the bar door, flipped his lock blade over to a natural grip and slashed at the twice-downed man five to seven times, scoring with about half the strokes. The defender made it to his feet again and ran out of sight with the knifer in close pursuit.

Gary learned nothing more about the incident or the outcome, except that the defender had been seeing the knifer's wife.

FATE OF 153 TARGETS OF BLADE AND SHANK ATTACKS (IN PERCENTAGES)

Target	% Deployment	ATTACKER Legal	KO'd	Maim	Dth.	Arm	Leg	Gut	Chest	Back	Neck	Head/ Face
Man	78	36	26	3	13	25	3	18	20	19	8	13
Woman	20	50	37	13	27	30	-	23	43	-	16	13
Child	2	67	67	-	67	33	-	-	33	-	67	33

* This indicates the percentage of victims who were injured in that location. Many victims sustain injuries to multiple locations.

The above table does not take into account the fate of those who attack knifers or those who engage in mutual combat with or against the blade.

• • •

My 9-year-old son, who computed the stats for this study, was very impressed by the number of back injuries suffered by men and was very pleased that his demographic only had a 2-percent risk of edged-weapon attack. He said, "Daddy, according to these numbers, there sure are a lot of stupid men out there."

ADDENDUM

The best in-depth examination of the personal characteristics that a fighter who wishes to function effectively and consistently in face-to-face blade confrontations must develop is *Gates of Fire* by Steven Pressfield (Bantam Books, 1999), a novel about the Spartans who fought the Persians at the Battle of Thermopylae.

Conclusion

A GRIM ECHO

I take you back to the midnight lunch for 12 grocery clerks in the lounge of a mega-supermarket (from Chapter 1). The diminutive Mole returned to his mates a hero, after cowing the rotund Jet in the men's room—with the aid of my Othello.

There was much backslapping and other forms of manly praise for Mole, who was finally one of the guys and a man to be reckoned with. This was a positive bonding experience for the whole crew at the expense of Jet, the lowly janitor. For a crew whose lunchroom topics of conversation ranged from who was going to get canned next to who would charge Robert Redford the least to sleep with his wife, any new diversion was positive.

As Jet emerged from the men's room and walked through the lounge, the conversation took a grisly turn. "What would you have done to him if he had fought ya, Mole?" asked Bill.

"Why, I would have cut him."

"How?" said Bobby.

"Cut his head off! After running him through, of course."

Amidst the laughter I noticed Vinnie—a powder cocaine addict who generally settled for a box of diet pills washed down with a warm coffee and a Pepsi chaser—shaking his head in grim contemplation. To my questioning nudge, he answered, "Imagine gettin' a blade through all that. Man, that would be some work! Just imagine that. What a mess that would be."

Imagine that.

—James LaFond

Apologies

When Theresa needed a big brother, I was either beating a punching bag, crafting homemade weapons, stalking some hapless kid who had insulted my honor, or fulfilling some other ultramanly role.

The last time Cindy needed an attentive husband, chances are I was talking to a compulsive fighter about his most recent altercation or to somebody who was in the wrong place, at the wrong time, for the wrong reason, with the wrong people—or I was lost in thought, trying to make sense of it all.

Sorry, girls.

GLOSSARY OF
Slang Terms

I trust that the reader is well versed in standard American slang. Therefore, this reader's aid is intended to deepen understanding of African-American slang. Throughout this book, I have quoted various Ebonics speakers at length. Although I am neither black nor a linguist, I have had much experience translating and transcribing the speech of my black friends and subjects, resulting in a better-than-average grasp of Ebonics.

There are three Ebonics dialects currently spoken in Baltimore: *rural* (or southern), *urban*, and *contemporary*.

Rural Ebonics—spoken by Kenneth and Haynes—has a lyrical quality well suited for emotional storytelling. Speakers may use standard English for context and background.

Urban Ebonics—spoken by Sandman, Krazee Shank KillPower, SmackDaddy Jay, Bubba Crank, and MumbleJack—is the least broken and blandest dialect, being a hybrid or rural ebonics and industrial American slang. It exhibits a strong tendency toward abbreviation.

Contemporary Ebonics, or "yo-talk"—spoken by Spin and YoMan—is a kind of cant (secret language) featuring a limited and contrived vocabulary heavily dependent on tone, gesture, and the use of yo as a noun, pronoun, verb, adverb, or adjective.

I have recorded all the above terms in context during the compilation of the Violence Index.

bitch—black female
brutha—fellow victim of white racism
cave boy—white male street person
chili-peppa—Hispanic person
chyle—child
"Come see me!"—challenge to mortal combat
cracka—white person
crazy—dangerous enough to depend on
crib—residence
da joint—jail or prison
five-O—police
groans—testicles (multidescriptive for sex and violence)
ho—prostitute
krazee—too dangerous to hang with
lady—white female
nigga—reasonable black person
nigger—mean, lowdown, unreasonable black person
nine—shoot to kill, as in "Nine 'im with yo tirty-eight!"
offa (offrin')—criminal charge
ranch—gang hangout (not hideout)
serious strapped—heavily armed
The Man—mythic embodiment of white race conciseness
yo—you, your, yours, him, hello, listen, what?, me
Yo—my special friend

About the
Author

James LaFond works as a night laborer in Baltimore, where he has been documenting the violent underside of the human population and the relationship of ordinary aggression to the hysteria of contemporary martial arts study since 1966. His wife, Cindy, pays the life insurance bill well in advance of the due date.

The Violence Project is an ongoing effort by the author. If you would like to know more about it or add your violent experiences to his databank, please write to him in care of Paladin Press (Gunbarrel Tech Center, 7077 Winchester Circle, Boulder, CO 80301).